The Great Unlearning

Books by Mary La

Fear Means Go - Poems and Photography

Enduring Love - Inspiring Stories of Love and Wisdom at the End of Life

www.Mary-La.com

The Great Unlearning

A unique memoir of inspiring self-portraits and incredible, true stories of transcendence

Mary La

LaRui Press, Ashland, Oregon

The Great Unlearning
A unique memoir of inspiring self-portraits
and incredible, true stories of transcendence

by Mary La
© 2022 Mary La
Published by LaRui Press, Ashland, Oregon

All rights reserved. No part of this book may be used or reproduced by any means without the written permission of the publisher except in the case of brief quotations embodied in critical articles and reviews.

Editor: Deborah Mokma, booksavvystudio.com

Book & Cover Design: Chris Molé, booksavvystudio.com

ISBN: 978-0-578-31452-5

First Edition
Printed in the United States of America

This is a work of creative nonfiction. The stories and dialogue in this book have been recreated from the author's recollection and perception of events and by interviews with family members. While all the stories in this book are true, some names, identifying details, and locations of events have been changed to protect the privacy of the people involved. Some content may be troubling for some readers, discretion is advised.

The Great Unlearning is dedicated to my
four-year-old self—innocent, joyous, and whole.
Welcome to my journey of finding her again.

Contents

Squirming Out of My Comfort Zone 1
Tree Heart 5

PART ONE: Remembering
    The Runaway 9
    The Unloved Daughter 15
    Belonging 21
    Fitting In 25
    On Guard 29
    Learning to Pretend 33
    Gullible Girl 37
    Girls Like Me 41
    Go Ask Your Mother 47
    It Was A Boy 53
    The Calling 59
    Me Too 69
    Murmuration 73
    The Myth of Me 77

PART TWO: Unlearning
    Dreadlocks 83
    Higher Selves 89
    Soul Retrieval 93
    Nathan Daniel 97
    Wounded Healer 101
    Walking on Eggshells 105
    Leap 111
    Men Like Him 117
    The Mystery 121
    Flaws 125

Hard as Nails 131
Wailyn 135
Need to be Needed.................................... 139
Busy Mind of a Queen Bee..................... 145
Carried Away 149
Overachiever 153
Imposter Syndrome................................. 157

PART THREE: Transcendence
Take Up Space... 161
To Be Vulnerable..................................... 165
Trust the Struggle 169
Subrosa 175
Calling in Joy 179
Running Out of Steam 183
Catharsis... 189
NESS.. 193
The Stages of Change 197
Trust Fall 201
Who I Am..205
Love is Not Enough 209
Falling into Love 213
Love Fully... 217
Bloom Where You Are Planted............. 221
How to Save a Life 225
The Second Beginning............................229

About the Author 230

Squirming Out of My Comfort Zone

Some part of my story might be yours as well, and if you are someone who has experienced trauma, this book is for you. With it, may you find yourself in a perfect environment to unlearn and be guided onto a triumphant path to healing.

Welcome to *The Great Unlearning*, my uncensored journey to remembering, unlearning, and transcendence through inspiring conceptual self-portraits and incredible true stories.

I created this book for my own self-discovery, as well as to facilitate the healing and transformation of old limiting belief systems and habits forged in order to survive traumatic, life-altering experiences of my formative and adolescent years.

Initially, while writing this book, I was unable to find any evidence of what it was that held me together during the traumas of my life, and I have no memory of any conscious determination pulling me through to the other side of adversity. It appears that I've made it to the well-grounded, happy place I am in now thanks to the discovery of the secret to perseverance—in spite of having never been given the tools to keep going when I was a wounded kid (and adult).

I approached writing about my traumatic childhood cautiously, with the understanding that it could rear up and bite me, which it did many times during the two years it took me to complete this book. While the process did indeed trigger painful memories I hadn't visited in years, it also opened a door that could never be closed again. Although the writing of my stories caused me to relive much of the anguish I had previously suffered, by doing so, those experiences have finally become my past.

When I learned that the damaging aftermath of my distorted worldview was responsible for the poor choices I made as an adult, and that those choices were directly related to my childhood trauma, my entire outlook changed dramatically. An intense curiosity about the early stages of my wounding and how it had shaped my view of the world led me to feeling courageous enough to fully embrace the memories of my past, which subsequently

healed some of the deepest cuts and awakened me to the beautiful potential contained in allowing myself to be vulnerable. Telling my stories has also provided me with freedom from shame and regret for anything I did or did not do.

I am a resilient success story.

Through the writing of my stories, and creating the art for this book, I was able to uncover the roots of my suffering, and the origins of my values and irrational self-perceptions were revealed— as well as the ways in which my childhood wounding bled into my motives for disastrous decisions made as teenager and adult. Further, learning what needs had not been met as a child provided me with permission to finally ask for what I need, which was followed by an exquisite abundance of love and support. In learning the reasons for having developed self-destructive coping mechanisms, I could finally let them go; and by confronting and unlearning old ways of being that no longer served me, or anyone around me, I was able to make some sense of the life I have lived so far.

While *The Great Unlearning* is a safe harbor for the most challenging and painful stories of my life, this book also contains inspiring stories and conceptual self-portraits which illustrate my often cathartic processes in breaking through to living a life of healthy value-driven choices, joyous purpose, and self-love.

While writing my most difficult stories, I worked hard to detach from fear of judgment and rejection in order to share the absolute truth of what I had discovered during this transformative evolution, although the fact that the painful and exuberant unraveling of my life so far would be witnessed by readers provided a powerful momentum for me to candidly express vulnerability in my words and photographs.

The Great Unlearning is for people who are arriving at a time in their life when they are ready for a catalyst for change. It is my intention that my memoir will offer readers courage and permission to take a similar leap of faith into bold exploration of their own life-defining experiences so they can bravely examine what it is that prevents the expression of their most authentic self—and to take creative risks for what they love and believe in. With creativity a continuous source of healing for me, I know it can be for others too.

Some part of my story might be yours as well, and if you are someone who has experienced trauma, this book is for you. With it, may you find yourself in a perfect environment to unlearn and be guided onto a triumphant path to healing.

This book also contains inspiring stories and conceptual self-portraits which illustrate my often cathartic processes in breaking through to living a life of healthy value-driven choices, joyous purpose, and self-love.

Tree Heart

My daughter shed some beautiful and relatable light on topics such as self-worth, being enough, shame, identity, coping, self-care, vulnerability, self-sacrifice, and boundaries.

I'd like to introduce my younger daughter, now twenty-nine, who has contributed to the potency of this book in many surprising and transformative ways. My daughter says she was born an old lady, which I believe, because she has a mature wisdom about her that a master's degree in mental health counseling has only magnified. Having succeeded in the goal of becoming the counselor she didn't have while navigating her own turbulent adolescent waters, she is an advocate for underserved populations at a university, where she inspires struggling students while helping them realize their own worth and make the best educational choices.

After offering to consult with me about emotional health, my daughter shed some beautiful and relatable light on topics such as self-worth, being enough, shame, identity, coping, self-care, vulnerability, self-sacrifice, and boundaries. Her scholarly and intuitive advice helped me identify and explore core issues that I was writing about. For example, I would ask her questions about how self-worth and shame develop, why people avoid conflict, or what kinds of experiences shape identity. Her answers were always brilliant, to the point, and very practical.

This is the child who, at age five, drew me the scene of her birth on a napkin with a crayon and told me about *Isabella*, her guardian angel, who had told her she would be safe coming into the world. She was spot on as she described the bright lights in the birthing room, the furniture placement, where the window was, and the cold air she felt when she was born.

And she has been giving me sound advice since she was about six years old. One evening when I came home late from work, dinner was going to be delayed, and I was a little irritated. She noticed my frustration and calmly patted the kitchen chair next to her as she lovingly said, "Mom, you sound upset, please sit down, right here."

Once we were seated, she gave me her undivided attention and offered me an opportunity to share what was on my mind. I didn't want to burden this beautiful child with my adult problems, but her heartfelt gesture was enough to make me stop and take a deep breath. With a shift in attitude, I sat down next to her, pulled her onto my lap, wrapped my arms around her gorgeous self, and we proceeded to giggle together about the happy highlights of her day while the pasta water came to a boil. She helped me with dinner, and we got it to the table on time.

The world needs the opportunity to hear, and heal, from what this young woman has to share.

Along with my wish that the stories and art in this book provide a service to audiences ready to connect with a deeper truth and hope for healing, it is my plan to share what I've learned about transcending a traumatic childhood in inspiring presentations alongside my daughter, who has helped clarify many of the concepts contained in these pages.

The world needs the opportunity to hear, and heal, from what this young woman has to share.

PART ONE
Remembering

The Runaway

MY FATHER ASKED MY FIVE BROTHERS AND SISTERS and I to line up against the wall in the dining room, he had something important to tell us. The five o'clock news blared from our giant box of a TV as two reporters had an emotional conversation about a nineteen-year-old girl named Patricia who had been kidnapped by the Symbionese Liberation Army, although to me, what my father was about to say was far worse.

He slowly sat down in one of our rickety wooden dining chairs, landing with his elbows on his knees. My father was only weeks into recovering from a second heart attack, an experimental triple bypass heart surgery, and a consequent infection from a tainted blood transfusion—all after just turning forty.

Silently looking up at us with a furrow in his brow as deep as the resentment I had brewing for being a kid in my crappy world, he bought himself a few moments by lighting up a Pall Mall nonfilter cigarette and taking a long, slow drag. After picking off a piece of tobacco from his tongue while holding in the smoke that would eventually kill him, the muscles in his jaw pulsated while billows of smoke streamed through his flared nostrils like an angry bull. Then, in a choking voice, he finally spoke. "I have some bad news for you guys. Your mother left on a long vacation. I don't know if she is coming back."

My mother had walked out on our family of eight to go to Hawaii with a guy named Bob.

Her timing was horrendous. She was done. She didn't say *goodbye, I love you, good luck*, or anything. The second eldest of six kids, at fourteen I already had a hundred holes in my heart, had not yet won her love, and now felt clear that I never would.

This was the beginning of my childhood hell breaking loose.

It was many years before my mother told my younger sister she had made special sack lunches for us on the day she left, each containing a rare and coveted Twinkie. She said she believed it would be the last time she would ever do this chore, confessing that if she didn't leave when she did, "Someone would have gotten hurt or killed." I've often wondered if she was one of those mothers who could have snapped, perhaps making headlines by driving us six kids off a cliff buckled into our seats.

With our mother never having been a source of positive, loving guidance in our lives, there was a general sense of elation from my siblings, the youngest being six, who were thrilled to have our fun-loving father all to themselves. I took the news differently, and felt personally abandoned without a lick of motherly guidance about boys, or how to take care of myself. The numbness that crept in behind my eyes would cloud every decision I'd make for the next twenty years.

I didn't like much about myself in those days, and feeling like a victim, was lonely and quite angry with no healthy way to express it. My already meager self-esteem and poor self-confidence made me a bright and shiny target for bullies, and easy prey for parasitic exploiters who take advantage of people lacking moral guidance or boundaries.

I began gravitating to any person or group that would give me attention, and soon chose to

With many challenging and uncomfortable experiences awaiting me, I took near fatal risks and made uninformed decisions with disastrous consequences that I've kept secret until now.

---

numb out with alcohol, drugs, and the wrong crowds. With many challenging and uncomfortable experiences awaiting me, I took near fatal risks and made uninformed decisions with disastrous consequences that I've kept secret until now.

My siblings and I didn't band together as some families do under circumstances like these. For me, life became an irritating game of competitive and chaotic musical chairs, with someone always coming in last, thus missing out on a safe place to land and losing their place in line for the limited support available.

Despite my father's physical weakness and fatigue, he rallied us with pep talks about the importance of family and sticking together. He dubbed our motherless clan *The Monroe Brothers*, the origin of which is unclear, but to this day, if any of us kids need help in anyway, the Monroe Brothers will mobilize to help. Doing his best to make this unstable time fun for us, he named our kitchen *The Starlite Café*, and delegated all of us jobs to keep the house running as best we could.

Floundering in a hormonally driven rebellious phase, I didn't want much to do with family bonding, preferring instead to zone out while listening to Pink Floyd's new album, *Dark Side of the Moon*, or smoking my father's cigarettes in the bathroom while blowing the smoke up into the fan to avoid being caught.

My father began dating a wiry, chain-smoking woman named Iris who was often in the house, and who stabbed us all in the back with her deceitful behaviors, resulting in our referring to her as "Iris the Bitch." She was mean-spirited and didn't appear to like children.

When I turned sixteen, Iris told me if I moved out, my father would have enough money to get another lifesaving heart surgery. She also asked my older brother Allan to leave. I later learned there was no such surgery in store for him, she just wanted fewer kids receiving the attention she coveted from my father. Within a few months, as eleventh grade began, I received a GED, which meant I had completed high school, and I moved into a studio apartment. After lying my way into a job as a secretary at a legal firm, I later learned it was the same firm that was representing my mother in her nasty divorce from my father.

My father realized he couldn't run the house and manage four remaining children with his current state of health and

finances; his social security and GI benefits weren't enough to support a family while paying my mother alimony. He couldn't go back to work as a grocery store manager because of his poor health, and tried mowing lawns for our neighbors, but nearly collapsed with fatigue in doing so. At this point, he had me ask my mother to move back in to take care of my younger brothers and sisters, which she did, bringing along her new husband, Nicholas, a Frenchman who was an engineer at Lockheed. When she and Nicholas moved in, my father spent a couple of weeks living in his fifteen-year-old Lincoln Continental, essentially homeless, before moving in with Iris the Bitch, after which he filed for bankruptcy to wipe out his medical bills.

On Tuesdays my father would make the rounds, picking up all us kids, and we'd eagerly pile into his squeaky cream-colored ship of a Lincoln for our weekly "Big D Day" adventures. The "D" stood for donuts with dad. He was loving, goofy, compassionate, and very kind. On one such day, my sister Ann spilled an entire soda in the back seat of his car, at which my father nonchalantly waved his hand in the air from the driver's seat, and without looking back at her simply said, "Don't worry about it honeybun, it will soak in."

During this period, when my father had one of his frequent hospitalizations for heart failure, my mother stormed into his hospital room and yanked the oxygen off his face, exclaiming, "You can't buy love with donuts!" But our father did *not* buy love with donuts. He bought us donuts while he was loving us.

At twenty, I made the decision to move to Hawaii, wanting some distance from the brutal consequences of my teenage years in California. Stopping by the family home to say goodbye to my siblings, I noticed a framed cover of *Time* on the wall between their two bedrooms which featured a grim photo of dead bodies sprawled out on a walkway and a field. The image of a large rusty vat of purple liquid filling the foreground contained the words *The Cult of Death*, and referred to an article about the Jonestown Massacre. When I asked my mother about it, she mumbled something about lack of gratitude and how we take life for granted, which seemed to confirm that moving away was the right thing for me to do, although I also felt guilty for not staying to protect my younger siblings. I think, however, that if I had stayed I might have gotten hurt—or worse.

Over the next few years, while I was enjoying life in Hawaii, my mother kicked the remaining kids out of the house, one by one, typically by the time they were nearing sixteen. My sister Vicki was notified to get out by a note on the bathroom mirror written in red lipstick; Ann's turn came when she gave thanks to God, instead of my mother's husband Nicholas, for putting dinner on the table. After grabbing Ann's plate of spaghetti, then dumping it out onto the front lawn, my mother gave her back the empty plate and said, "Here, have God fill it." My brother Eddie, with no place to go when he was told to leave, slept either in my mother's car in the driveway or in the snack shack at the Little League baseball field. My brother George was the last kid in the house when my mother went through the legal process of emancipating him at fourteen so she would no longer be held responsible, or be required to provide him with any support. Thankfully, all five siblings eventually found their way into lifestyles and relationships that kept them at a safe distance from our mother's reach.

The day before my father's fifty-fifth birthday, he had his last heart attack at his home in California, dying shortly after arriving at the hospital. In my mid-twenties at the time, this news arrived on the morning of an anatomy and physiology final at the University of Hawaii, where I was a pre-med major with the goal of becoming a doctor.

The Unloved Daughter

The absence of any female heroes growing up required that I become a hero for myself, and for my daughters. A mother unlike my own in a million ways, I have broken the cycle that my mother, her mother, and her mother's mother were trapped in.

I have no memories of being loved by my mother. No sweet recall of warm moments being cuddled on her lap as she stroked my hair and told me how much she loved me. I've always wondered what that would feel like.

I did feel special the day I ran through a sliding glass door, however, when I was ten. My older brother was pulling the wings off of a live monarch butterfly in the backyard, and as I attempted to run into the house to have my mother make him stop, instead ran face first into the sliding glass door. After shattering the glass, I collapsed on the threshold, halfway in, bloodied from cuts all over my face and body. The tip of my broken nose, nearly sliced off, was hanging by a thread of skin. When my mother ran in from the kitchen, she grabbed my shoulders, then dragged me over the broken glass just far enough in to avoid the rest of the door which quickly came crashing down like a guillotine. My butterfly torturing brother took off his boy scout belt, buckled it tight around my left arm to stop the blood from spurting from my left wrist, and my parents took me to the hospital where they doted on me in a way I'd never experienced before. I felt like it was worth all the stitches to my face, shoulder, and wrist as they hovered over me, even buying me ice cream on the way home. It was a weird kind of heaven.

Later that year, my brother got his turn. After receiving a hand grenade from a neighbor who was a WWII vet, he stuffed the grenade full of match heads to make a smoke bomb. I remember him showing it off in the house as all of my siblings took turns playing with it, after which it unexpectedly exploded while he was out on our driveway and blew most of his right hand off. The blast shattered the windows in the front of the house, shredding the laundry hanging from the open garage door, and loaded his thirteen-year-old body with shrapnel. He got ice cream on the way home from the hospital too.

I mostly remember my mother's irritability, and her frequent preoccupation with something that made her eyebrows knit together. It was hard not to rub her the wrong way, so I stayed out of her way as best I could. We all grew to fear her, and it took some courage to ask for what we needed because it could feel like we were intruding on her space. She would often whip her body around, arms raised in the air as she shouted, "What?!" before locking eyes with our terrified faces as her hands landed on her hips. When she was really angry, she would yell, "red light!" At that point we knew we had to stop what we were doing, go to our rooms, and be quiet until we heard "green light."

Our family of eight lived in a small three-bedroom house in a typical suburban development in southern California. I shared a bedroom with my two sisters; the three boys were across the hall. On any given day, we were each only allowed to go in and out of the house twice because the screen door slammed with ear splitting precision and interrupted my mother's concentration. Six kids and more than twelve slams were a minimum for a "red light" afternoon. At bedtime, my mother would usher us all down the hall into our rooms and stand in the doorway to make sure we were in bed. After turning off the light, she'd twirl the glowing ember of her cigarette in the air over her head a few times to entertain us before closing the door. I don't remember any bedtime rituals of stories, getting tucked in, or personal hygiene (one of my sisters developed baby dreadlocks under her pelt of sandy blond hair). We all ran around with poop stains in our underwear and dirty rings around our necks and ankles.

While my brother was recovering from surgery to save the remainder of his hand, we had an epic "red light" day. My mother was so mad, she yanked dinner plates from the dishwasher and lifted them over her head before

sending them crashing to the kitchen floor, one by one, yelling about how sick and tired she was. As my siblings and I sat stunned at the picnic table we used in the kitchen, my youngest brother, who was in a highchair at the far end, started crying, which made matters worse.

My fear of her became permanent the day she yanked me from the backyard swing set, then dragged me into the house by my hair because she thought I had eaten the chocolate frosting off of my grandpa's birthday cake. Although I hadn't, she punished me for it anyway, angrily folding me over her lap and spanking me over and over—despite my screaming "red light" as loud and as many times as I could.

Although my mother didn't reveal her pain to us in understandable ways, I knew she had been raised by an angry mother whose mother had also been angry. Maybe my mother didn't know how to love because she'd never had love modeled for her?

Over time, after learning by her example that I was unlovable and not worthy of attention or affection, I accepted what appeared to be love from anyone who offered it as I grew up. Drifting through the unfortunate circumstances of my young life, because I lacked a positive self-image—an apparent consequence of not receiving love from one who should have provided it—I needed consistent external validation from wherever I could get it. And I found it alright, but at the expense of my physical and emotional wellbeing.

It's entirely possible my father wasn't the saint that my brothers, sisters, and I remember him as, since my relationship with him was completely different than the one he had with my mother. He was good at fathering, but perhaps not at being a husband. That was my mother's claim, anyway.

It is also possible that my mother had been in survival mode, doing the best she could at treading the waters of her own personal hell while being pregnant nearly every year for a decade (she had seven children, with the first born dying at birth). With a growing number of toddlers hanging onto her legs while she tried to keep her life together as an overextended housewife and mother, I was one of her irritating problems.

So, I was forced to mother myself into adulthood, something I was not very good at it. With all of the dysfunctional relationships I found myself in strikingly similar to the broken one I had with my mother, I wonder now if the selfless choices to please other people were subconsciously made to please her.

I blamed her out loud for quite a bit of my suffering, believing that my poor confidence and lack of self-esteem was her fault. During the years when I refused to forgive her, or even speak to her, I became stuck in a toxic resentment which was accompanied by a low, steady hum of anger that manifested in constant angst.

These descriptions of my mother are all from childhood memories, and even as I grew into adulthood, I could only see her through the lens of a neglected child. But after realizing I had become a different person, I began to think that perhaps she could be too, since after divorcing my father, two other men had found her lovable enough to marry later in life.

So, about fifteen years ago, I flew my mother to my home in Oregon with the intent of having a deep and meaningful conversation about my experience as her daughter growing up. I felt ready, thanks to a blossoming which followed years of excruciating inner work. After learning that my refusal to forgive was trapping me in an anger which prevented me from moving forward with an understanding of our relationship, I understood how blaming her made it hard for me to be compassionate.

One day after she arrived, we were alone in my kitchen talking about our life in California, skirting the periphery of my childhood pain, when I nervously wrapped my arms around her and found the courage to whole-heartedly say, "I forgive you." I felt triumphant, and as a moment of silence passed, teared up with a sense of joy. But when she broke away from my hug with a puzzled look on her face and asked, "For what?" it appeared she might not think she had done anything to warrant forgiveness, or perhaps didn't quite understand how her mothering continued to affect me even as an adult.

Regardless, my lower lip started to quiver, and feeling my heart flop in my chest, I slowly turned away so she wouldn't see my face as I went to the kitchen sink and held on. The color in my cheeks drained down my body to my sweaty feet, as did my courage to continue the conversation. My well of grief no longer seemed worth diving into with her as I resigned myself to—

After learning that my refusal to forgive was trapping me in an anger which prevented me from moving forward with an understanding of our relationship, I understood how blaming her made it hard for me to be compassionate.

and am still recovering from—the likelihood of never having a loving relationship with her.

After one of my sisters gave birth to her first child, our mother had burdened her with some brutal honesty by telling her, "I never really wanted to be a mother" and, "Children don't become a joy until they turn eighteen." But these sentiments had landed on our tender young hearts decades before she said this out loud.

It is my prediction that my father was correct when he said to my mother before he died, "You are going to die a lonely old woman." She doesn't have loving relationships with any of her children or grandchildren, with a couple of my siblings tolerating her, at best.

The absence of any female heroes growing up required that I become a hero for myself, and for my daughters. A mother unlike my own in a million ways, I have broken the cycle that my mother, her mother, and her mother's mother were trapped in.

As a hospice nurse, a ping of envy tightens my throat when I see a devastated daughter at the bedside of her beloved dying mother. But perhaps I've been spared the despair of losing a dear mother, with my own already feeling dead to me, even though she is living in New Mexico. Or maybe Texas.

I prioritize and support my daughters with all of my heart, and can't imagine not being in their lives. I offer those darlings unconditional love in every way I can, joking with them that I would drive to Africa in a car without air conditioning if they needed to be rescued. They know I would come get them in the middle of the night, anywhere, no questions asked. All they have to say is, "Mom, I'm in Africa, I need you," and I'll be on my way to wherever they are.

I feel deep sadness that my mother has missed out on my most rich and amazing life. She doesn't know the brilliance and beauty of her accomplished granddaughters, who live lives in their fullest expression of joy and service to humanity. Both of my daughters have gifted me the greatest compliment by saying, on many occasions: "Mom, I hope I turn out just like you."

Belonging

My interests took a turn toward a type of survival I wasn't fit for, and I became lost without a touchstone to help me feel safe.

As a kid, I never truly felt like I belonged anywhere, and felt treated differently, though I was not completely sure why. In elementary school, when my siblings and I were issued round wooden tokens to give to the lunch lady for our noon time meal, we had to stand in a separate line along the scuffed wall of the cafeteria with the "poor kids."

In that large, echoey room smelling of sour milk cartons and canned spaghetti sauce, no matter what was on the menu we didn't get the same hot food as the other kids, and our cold lunches came in a small brown box that always seemed greasy, despite the packaged food inside. I never felt I belonged with the poor kids, it seemed like a mistake. Although we also wore secondhand clothes, my skin color was different than theirs, and most of those kids didn't speak English, so I didn't know how to speak to them. Trying not to radiate my embarrassment, with eyes firmly planted on my shoes, I'd hide behind my long stringy blond hair as the line slowly moved along.

For reasons unknown to me, I went straight from first grade to a class mixed with third and fourth graders. Although I easily kept up with the older kids in reading, writing, and math, I felt out of place as a younger kid in an older blended classroom. In addition, nobody wanted to be my friend, which was probably because I ruled the playground during group calisthenics, when I could jump higher, and run faster, than anyone else.

On the days with no sack lunch from home, I'd skip eating because I didn't want to be perceived as—or feel—different standing in the poor kids line. I would go out on the playground and play tether ball alone, often with a ferocity that made the boys take notice. During recesses, when a few brave kids stepped into my little painted circle on the asphalt, I got good at unabashedly wrapping that ball fast and tight up on the pole, out of reach to any opponent who tried to take me on. Undefeated, I was teased by the boys for being strong, while the girls called me a tomboy. Having scored highest in the fifth grade for the Presidential Physical Fitness award, I cherished the red, white, blue and gold embroidered patch I'd proudly earned, and the certificate signed by President Nixon. But this achievement only fueled more teasing from the kids at school who weren't fit enough to participate, and the kids who couldn't even do one pull up called me a freak. I had thought I would be liked if I was a good athlete, but nope, at least not in the fifth grade.

In sixth grade, the teacher would choose a "secretary" each week to sit at a desk next to his, facing the classroom. This lucky girl would proudly collect and hand out papers, erase the chalk board, and tidy up the classroom. When he asked me to be his secretary, I couldn't believe it, and actually felt chosen. But my fleeting sense of worthiness only lasted until the mean girls in class let everyone know I didn't I deserve it. Pinching their noses and teasing me about deodorant and showering, you'd think I would get the hint that I had poor personal hygiene, but I didn't. I stunk. Plus, I beat them all in tetherball, and they didn't like that one bit. I declined the offer to be the class secretary that week, not wanting any more attention, but I got it anyway.

I would fantasize about blending in at the long lunch table by the window in the cafeteria, longing to sit with those giggly girls with pretty hair, clean clothes, and black and white saddle shoes; the girls who often brought their lunches from home in cheerfully printed white paper lunch bags brimming with bologna sandwiches on Wonder Bread, little bags of potato chips, and Twinkies. Although I looked like them, because I didn't have the same clothing and mannerisms as they did, they bullied me into believing I wasn't worthy of their prissy company. When they pointed their fingers at me while laughing at my gangly features and how I dressed, I felt I would never be as good as them, or anyone like them, and it didn't seem worth trying. I was a poor kid who didn't understand what that really meant, all I knew was how it felt.

What I was learning was that being different meant I was an unlovable freak: I was a freak as a younger kid in older classes, I played tetherball like a freak, and I could do sit-ups freakishly fast. Having been told that enough times, I came to believe it.

In middle school, encouraged by my father to check out a community track and field club, I got a pair of big clunky athletic shoes and started running cross country. I enjoyed running around town, which became a way to get places and blow off steam, but this too wasn't perceived as a normal thing to do where I lived, and people let me know as much.

My father had been a pole vaulter in college, and when I showed promise in jumping events, he bought a high jump kit and put it in our backyard. After mastering the Fosbury Flop and beating most kids by a couple of inches, I went on to try every track and field event. One season, unable to decide on just one or two, my event became the decathlon. With special rigid white track shoes that had different sized cleats screwed into the soles for each event, I finally felt like I belonged. I started winning ribbons, traveling all over southern California for track meets, and even ran with Mary Decker once, who went on to become a world record holder in the mile. She inspired me to run even harder.

I also tried out for the drill team, and got in. We marched in local parades with the middle school band and wore little red sailor minidresses with big white collars. I was good at choreographing precision group dance routines while we waved flags and tipped our sailor hats at the spectators. Proud to be part of the team, I felt like I was contributing to something good.

But my enthusiasm in drill team and running came to a screeching halt when my mother left our family. When she abandoned me, I abandoned any semblance of worthiness. I quit running, discovered cigarettes, and was soon busted in the school bathroom for smoking, resulting in being kicked off the drill team the morning of a big school performance that I had choreographed two dances for. I sat in the audience, humiliated. After this, my interests took a turn toward a type of survival I wasn't fit for, and I became lost without a touchstone to help me feel safe.

Fitting In

I wasn't actually intending to die that day, although my silent screams for attention could have gone terribly wrong. My desire was only to kill myself "just enough" to impress a gang of ninth grade kids at school.

I sliced into my wrists with a razor-sharp edge of a broken Coke bottle while sitting cross-legged in my driveway, careful not to sit on the oil stains where my mother used to park her car. It was a sunny Thursday afternoon in April of 1974 when I broke that bottle on the warm cement in front of my bare feet, the pain of slowly cutting into my wrists was more intoxicating than alarming. As little crimson pearls oozed out of my fresh cuts, I felt disappointed when blood didn't spurt out onto the ground.

But just as the blood began dripping down my arms, my older brother walked out our front door. Quickly sucking the blood from my wrists, I crossed my arms so he wouldn't see the fresh wounds. When he sat down next to me and asked what I was doing, distractedly rummaging through his backpack, I lied and said I was waiting for someone to come over.

I wasn't actually intending to die that day, although my silent screams for attention could have gone terribly wrong. My desire was only to kill myself "just enough" to impress a gang of ninth grade kids at school. This collection of delinquents would sit in a circle in the garage of a vacant house in my neighborhood on Copper Avenue, and had included a boy who committed suicide because his mother shaved his head as punishment for stealing candy from the Stop and Go—a convenience store a few blocks from my house where my father once worked. The fourteen-year-old boy had effectively cut his wrists with his father's straight edge razor, and the gang revered him as some kind of hero for taking such a bold action of defiance.

The girls in this gang were known as the *tough chicks*. I frequently crossed paths with one of them after school, who often smoked a cigarette while waiting for her ride in the parking lot. Strikingly confident and daring in the way she carried herself, I would have given anything to be like her.

Walking past her one afternoon, after she gave me a quick glance of acknowledgement with a serious lift of her chin, I felt "seen" by her. This was soon followed by an urgency to be accepted by her group. Willing to harm myself to accomplish this goal, my intention was to make a statement in order to appear worthy, and to prove my bravery. I bought the Coke from Stop and Go, and drank it while walking home.

The day after cutting my wrists, I positioned myself so the tough chick from the parking lot could see me with the loads of white gauze I had wrapped around my wrists to get her attention. When she asked me what happened, I lied with an outward confidence I didn't feel, and the bandages bought me an opportunity to be introduced to the gang later that afternoon.

As a rite of passage into this group, after being handed a brand-new No. 2 pencil, I was instructed to erase all layers of skin on the top of my left hand in a one-inch strip until it bled. Although my hand felt like I was lighting it on fire, my determination to fit in didn't allow me to stop mid-way and be perceived as a coward. When two drops of blood landed on my left shoe, I was told I had one more initiation to ride out.

One of the tough chicks stood behind me with her arms wrapped uncomfortably tight around my waist, then told me to hyperventilate before squeezing me as hard as she could. My upper body flailed forward as directed, and I passed out for a long minute before waking up on the floor—accepted. I was then given the task of stealing cigarettes from my parents as a fee for the next gathering.

The Copper Gang soon became my source of self-esteem, and I felt comfort being included in this group of misfits, although I couldn't identify with their anger and gutsy brazenness.

Over the next few weeks we played Spin the Bottle, other kissing games, and Seven Minutes in Heaven in a musty utility closet in the vacant garage. When I was paired up in the closet with a pimply boy with mushy McDonald's French fries stuck in his braces, and almost intolerable body odor, I shrieked as his ice-cold fingers found their way up my shirt. Everyone on the other side of the closet door laughed out loud, but I loved the attention, which I wasn't getting anywhere else.

With reluctance, I agreed to take a large grocery store paper bag full of marijuana home with me for two weeks to keep it "safe." I felt elated the gang found me dependable with their stash, though I never smoked the stuff, and wasn't interested in doing so. On the day I was supposed to bring it back to the circle, after retrieving it from under a pile of laundry in my closet, I opened my bedroom window, pried off a corner of the screen, then dropped the bag into the backyard. Nervously taking my first step toward calmly walking through the house before running around back to get the bag, a deep masculine voice yelled, "Busted!" and I yelped a newly learned cuss word as I was certain the police were in my backyard. Anxiously peeking out the window, and seeing it was one of my brothers intercepting the bag as it hit the ground, I quickly offered him a handful of the marijuana if he'd promise not to tell. But looking in the bag he declined, seeing mostly twigs which were not worth smoking, as he knew about these things.

Feeling like I had just finished an important job, I brought the bag of twiggy weed back to the circle. In exchange, I was given a small plastic baggie of crushed white pills one of the gang members took for his attention deficit disorder, and was instructed to stand on a corner by Safeway to wait for a high school boy in a black truck who would pay five dollars for the bag. The transaction went off without a hitch. I had no clue if it had contained any risk, and no part of me ever felt like I was in danger. I proudly handed over the five dollar bill and felt exuberant for pleasing the gang.

The next week, when the gang discussed plans to bully a special needs kid in the neighborhood, I found the courage to disagree with their intent, and was instantly not one of them anymore. After calling me a wimp, they kicked me out of the gang, and I was quickly replaced by a gullible middle schooler desperate to fit in.

The story I told myself was that I was rejected for speaking up for what I believed in, so why bother speaking up at all?

On Guard

All I could do was squeeze my eyes shut and tense my body for the possibility of a blow. I didn't know how to defend myself, but couldn't run away either because her threats were paralyzing.

I went to two different high schools in one school year, and was tormented by three Cholas at the first one. Although they never hurt me, they threatened to, especially after PE class. I would change into my street clothes in a bathroom stall in the girl's locker room, then stay there until I was sure the room was empty. It was the only place I felt safe. Even though I didn't make any noise, and held my breath as much as possible, I still feared I would be detected because my heart seemed to be pounding so loudly in my chest. I timed my safe exit by running to my next class and landing in my seat just as the bell was ringing.

I always felt the need to be on guard.

Their unkind words and body language had such power over me. All it took was one word, a sound, or a mean look tossed my way to make me cower. I felt inferior to them, and they knew it. I spent a couple of months hiding from them, but I knew where they were at all times. I could finally exhale when I saw their big brothers pick them up from school in their shiny Chevy Impala lowriders, bouncing all over the parking lot on their way out to the street with their speakers blaring a type of soulful Hispanic music.

The most loud-spoken of the three tormenting Cholas wrongly accused me of stealing her boyfriend. At fifteen, she wore bright red lipstick, heavy eye makeup, and big gold hoop earrings like my mother wore. One day, she rushed me after class, stood toe to toe with me, and rammed her forehead into mine as she threatened to beat me up.

All I could do was squeeze my eyes shut and tense my body for the possibility of a blow. I didn't know how to defend myself, but couldn't run away either because her threats were paralyzing. I had no idea who her boyfriend was, I didn't have one, and didn't want one. She probably didn't have any power in her life, so she had to

find it at school. I believe I was an easy target because I wasn't like them. Although my family lived in a school district that was predominantly Chicano, I was as white as the snow I saw in *National Geographic*.

I finally told my father about the Chola bullies at school and he had me transferred to a different high school without question— or any discussion on how to communicate with difficult people. But the new high school was full of surfers and stoners, so I was headed for trouble.

My fear of getting vicious attention from the Cholas, or anyone else for that matter, hung around my neck like a heavy weight for the next thirty years and manifested in painfully unexpected ways.

With very few boundaries, I set out to belong to whomever would have me. My ache for a sense of inclusion leaned me into anybody or any group that welcomed me and gave me attention. I set myself up for failure by learning how to pretend to be someone I wasn't, and soon gravitated toward a group of high school kids that liked to cut school, wander around town, and drink alcohol they swiped from their parent's liquor cabinets.

With very few boundaries, I set out to belong to whomever would have me. My ache for a sense of inclusion leaned me into anybody or any group that welcomed me and gave me attention.

Learning to Pretend

This experience colored my life like a dark purple bruise that wouldn't fade for decades.

I skipped ahead to the water's edge, then spun my body around in slow, blissful motion. Twirling, arms outstretched, I fingered the cool salty air of that beautiful March morning as my long blond hair floated effortlessly around my head, tickling my cheeks as a contented smile spread across my face. As my eyes closed, in total exhilaration of the moment I felt as free as a bird soaring along on an ocean breeze.

Although I was supposed to be in math class at my new high school, my three mentors at misbehaving had encouraged me to join them in a beach adventure instead of returning to school after lunch.

When one of these new classmates snapped a Polaroid of my joyous moment, I was abruptly pulled out of my happy twirl by the roar of their laughter. As their fingers pointed in my direction, the dizzy smile drained from my face upon hearing their dagger-like comments about how ugly I was in the photo.

"Your teeth are so crooked, Albino girl."

After critiquing the snapshot a bit more, they carelessly tossed it into the street as they walked toward a sandwich shop. Stunned and speechless, picking up the unflattering photo from the gutter, I had to agree with them wholeheartedly. Having confirmed I was ugly, they would of course leave me. Seeing myself in a repulsive light, and feeling unworthy of their friendship, this experience colored my life like a dark purple bruise that wouldn't fade for decades.

This day at the beach ignited my self-loathing beyond the smoldering embers of the typical adolescent body image issues I had been fanning since age ten. My self-hatred further fueled by bullies and teachers who were careless with their words and actions, the teasing I received for my gangly frame, freckles, poor hygiene, blond hair, breast size, and painful shyness caused me to feel different, and induced a deep

sense of shame. I soon developed significant social anxiety and a panic disorder that would nearly flatten me.

For the next few years, I learned to dumb down and up, depending on the situation I was idling in, a flexibility created by the fear of being rejected and left alone—or worse, disliked. Indeed, I adapted so well, I felt like an actress, able to blend in, or stand out. In reality, I was a *pretender*, doing my best to be accepted at all times.

At some pivotal moments in my near future, I took some naïve, dangerous, and often futile strides to be liked, loved, wanted, and needed. Trudging as blindly as I did through life, I'm surprised I made it out of my teenage years alive.

For the next few years, I learned to dumb down and up, depending on the situation I was idling in, a flexibility created by the fear of being rejected and left alone—or worse, disliked.

Gullible Girl

With bonfires and free flowing kegs of beer, some of the awkward edges came off my shy and distorted fifteen-year-old self-image which always seemed to chum around with me like a quiet evil twin.

Blossoming into looking decent in a bikini, the surfer crowd took me in for a summer. While I totally fit the part, with my stringy platinum blond hair covering most of my face, I didn't like surfing—and the wetsuits were bulky and unattractive—but I went to their beach parties anyway. With bonfires and free flowing kegs of beer, some of the awkward edges came off my shy and distorted fifteen-year-old self-image which always seemed to chum around with me like a quiet evil twin.

One day as I was tending to a hangover by getting a tan at a popular surfing spot, a man of about forty approached me with an offer to be a bikini model in a magazine. Super tan with weathered skin, his unruly mane of coarse brown hair had been bleached blond by saltwater and sun. Ecstatic at the thought he found me attractive enough to photograph caused me to think maybe I had been wrong about how I saw myself.

The next day, I got a ride five miles up the coast to meet the photographer at his home for the photoshoot, with my ride promising to pick me up two hours later. Excited about being chosen to be photographed for a magazine, I never thought to ask what magazine he was shooting for, or if he was going to pay me.

The photographer greeted me at the door, offered me some Champagne, and blew smoke in my face which I had heard was a sexy gesture, so I felt desired. While he fiddled with his camera out by the pool, I shuffled into his bathroom with my bag of clothes, make up, and a flute of the sweet bubbly goodness I'd never had before. Looking like I belonged in a rock band with lots of makeup and big ratty hair, I confidently headed out to the pool wearing an amber-beaded, crocheted string bikini bottom with matching halter top. He clicked away while telling me how pretty I was; so, feeling relaxed (and like a supermodel!) I puckered my lips and flung my long puffy blond hair around like I've seen women do in magazines.

Then, after giving me more Champagne, he had me lay on my side on a red velvet chaise lounge next to a palm tree. When he told me to untie my bikini bottom and let the beaded strings hang over my hip, woozy from the Champagne, I didn't hesitate. Instructing me to open up my bikini bottom and "touch" myself, I peeked at him through my big hair with a puzzled look, relaying the message that I didn't understand. Without taking the camera from his face he raised his voice, and said, "Put your fingers on your pussy!" in a demanding tone.

I obeyed him and quickly put my fingers between my open legs, not able to understand why he kept taking pictures even though I had grown tense and now had a bewildered look on my face.

When he then moaned, "Oh yah, baby, rub it," I thought *rub what*? Increasingly uncomfortable, I quickly tied my bikini bottom back up and saw his hand moving fast down into the crotch of his pants, confused about what he was doing I wondered if he had a wedgy he was trying to fix.

He appeared distracted by what was happening in his pants, so I stood up abruptly and told him I had to go. I'd never seen an erect penis before, and while I'd caught glimpses of my brother's little limp wieners, I'd never seen an adult man's in this condition.

As I hurried into the house to get my things from the bathroom, he came in after me, so I jumped into the shower and closed the frosted door. A blurry version of his naked body appeared in the doorway of the bathroom as he continued to stroke himself while breathlessly

A blurry version of his naked body appeared in the doorway of the bathroom as he continued to stroke himself while breathlessly promising he wouldn't hurt me.

---

promising he wouldn't hurt me if I came out of the shower and laid down on his bed. Not knowing what to say or do to defend myself against this man, I felt trapped, and started panicking and crying just as he shouted to God like he was in pain.

He finally stopped moving, slumped up against the bathroom wall for few seconds, then slowly walked out of the bathroom. After quickly getting dressed, I ran out of the house and down the hill of his street to wait for my ride, who was due to arrive at any moment.

Did I learn anything from that experience? Not really. I went on with my boundaryless life, setting myself up regularly for the potential of disaster.

Girls Like Me

Feeling nearly paralyzed, and quite disoriented as waves of chlorinated water splashed up onto my thighs, what happened next has haunted me for my entire life.

The security guard, firmly tapping my right foot with a scolding, "Shame on you," probably wanted to make sure I was conscious enough to know how she felt about my having just puked all over myself.

I was sprawled out on the concrete floor at my first rock concert somewhere in Los Angeles after having spent much of the show under the stadium stairs slumped up against a cinderblock wall, nearly unconscious, drenched in vomit. This sad situation began in the parking lot before the show when I had been offered a thermos of Tom Collins, my friends cheering me on as I guzzled the whole thing. It had been mostly gin, and as I stumbled into the stadium where Ted Nugent was to perform, my stomach violently churned while the venue spun. I tried to find a bathroom, but only got as far as hitting the wall next to its entrance, where I peed my pants, slid down onto my butt, and went in and out of consciousness.

When the memory of this senseless experience finally found its way to my adult mind, I wondered *why did I ever want to drink alcohol again?* But this was only the beginning of the journey of attempting to numb my pain.

Although I don't have many memories of being a high school student that fall, I remember snorting heroin off the hood of a root beer brown Karmann Ghia in a parking lot, and doing bong hits of marijuana laced with PCP—whatever that was. Every weekend I'd go to parties, naively accepting any drug or alcoholic drink that was offered. The feeling of not being in control was worth the feeling of being perceived as brave and accepted in a group. Any group. I'd do anything to be included.

Shortly after I got my driver's license, I tripped on LSD while driving to Inglewood to see an Eagles concert at the Forum. My father's old Lincoln miraculously had enough gas in it to get me and three of my stoned friends there and back without him knowing it. But when I rolled in at 2:00 am, seeing the light on in the kitchen and not wanting to get caught coming into the house high or discovered sleeping in my dad's car in the driveway, I chose to sleep in a filthy unlocked station wagon that was parked down the street. I never once considered what could have happened if someone hopped in that grimy junker of a car and sped off to some unsafe destination.

On another occasion, a biker gang scooped me up for a risky and exhilarating week after I accepted a ride home from the beach from a thirty-year-old bad boy on a Harley. Closing my eyes on the back of his hog, I relished long glorious hits of the woody smell of his leather jacket and the motor oil on his skin as we leaned into the turns of the windy roads in the coastal hills. Although I liked it when his loud and obnoxious friends called me *Puppy*, probably because I was by far the youngest of the bunch, when I refused to have sex with anybody, I was out.

My virginity was almost lost at a party in a dilapidated house in the suburbs of Los Angeles after snorting lines of cocaine on the polished cross section of a black rock with a bunch of dopeheads. I have no memory of how I got to this party, or when I came home—never being missed by my family meant it was easy to be gone. Around 1:00 am, I found myself in a bedroom with an older guy named Addison, who had to be at least twenty-five. We were naked in his twin bed, which felt like it was covered in a combination of sand and cracker crumbs. *Band on the Run* by Wings was stuck repeating on his record player, and his roommate was unconscious in a bean bag chair in the corner, most likely nearly overdosing from all the pills that were flying around that night. Addison was laying on top of me, jabbing my inner thigh with his stiff penis as his whiskery chin rubbed the skin nearly raw on my forehead. His long stinky brown hair tickled my cheeks, and continually found its way into my mouth. Tense and motionless, I lay there with my hands covering my face until he stopped poking my leg and asked if I was a virgin. When I squeaked out an embarrassing affirmative, he replied, "Save it for someone who loves you," then rolled off me and fell fast asleep.

Feeling harshly rejected, I thought he didn't like me enough to have sex with me. Although sixteen at the time, I really had no idea what love was, and thought it might be sex, yet wasn't even sure what happened during sex. Earlier that year, my mother had nonchalantly explained "A man will place his penis in your vagina," then mumbled something about a climax, followed by "I could really use a good fuck." I commiserated with a *me too*, yet didn't really know what I was concurring with. She took me to a bar the following weekend and offered pointers like, "Always get to know your bartender and tip well," and, "When you are out on a date, order a big salad so you can take the entrée home with you for lunch the next day."

Determined to be loved, I had sex (or maybe a fuck) for the first time with a boy named Jed a couple of weeks later. I was his first too. While it wasn't a beautiful and important moment, and we weren't in love, we were in the same place at the right time.

But having sex hadn't felt all that great, and I didn't understand why it was such a big deal since it was over in about a minute. I did learn, however, that all I had to do was lay there with my legs open, and bingo, I was worth something. I also learned the power of being sexy, and concluded sex wasn't for pleasure, it was for pleasing. My sexuality seemed to be the only thing of value because of the attention boys gave me if I behaved provocatively, and although I didn't always follow through, it sure felt good to be desired, even temporarily. I was like a heat seeking missile, looking for attention with a growing confidence that I could assume whatever shape was needed in order to fit in.

I was learning how to overcompensate and manipulate people into liking me, a skill that would serve me—and backfire too.

One of my girlfriends had wiggled herself in as a trophy girl at the local speedway, so I jumped on the same opportunity when it came my way. My job was to wear something sexy, ride sidesaddle on the back of a motorcycle once around the track, hop off seductively, then present the winner with a trophy and a kiss on the lips after the win was announced over the loudspeakers. With the moment of that kiss eliciting cameras flashing, loud cheers, and whistles in my direction, I was swallowed whole with the attention, believing I had something to do with the audience's excited response. How gullible I was back then. On this

The humiliation of this tragedy, which propelled me further into a self-loathing coma, would take a couple of decades to emerge from.

exciting evening, I was invited to join the speedway winner and his crew in a trailer after the press was finished taking pictures. Piled around a table with five boys that smelled of burning rubber and gasoline, I proceeded to get drunk on tequila. After reaching under the winner's shirt and unzipping his pants, I stroked his penis, something I had noticed boys doing to themselves. Having never done this before, I felt brave, daring, and quite innocent in doing so. Grabbing my wrist, the aroused winner tried to take me into the back of the trailer where he slept, but when I refused he said something about having blue balls, called me a "prick tease," and proceeded to kick me out.

A few weeks later, when I overheard another boy at a party also refer to me a prick tease, I still wasn't sure of its true meaning, but it didn't seem to matter at the moment because I was having fun. In fact, I felt a sense of satisfaction in learning there was a running bet between three boys about who could get me in the sack first. I was determined not to give any of them the pleasure of winning this bet, and it seemed to be nothing more than a fun game, until it turned disastrous.

These same boys may all have had sex with me a week later at a party when I took what I thought was a Quaalude, but was probably a Roofie, a mistake that was built to last. I must've been unconscious for about six hours, because the last thing I remembered was arriving at the party at 9:00 pm and taking a thick white pill with a whisky and 7UP. Upon awakening at 3:00 am, I found myself lying naked on my back in wet grass, feet dangling in a below ground hot tub. Feeling nearly paralyzed, and quite disoriented as waves of chlorinated water splashed up onto my thighs, what happened next has haunted me for my entire life: A boy I didn't recognize was standing in the hot tub, holding my legs open, and thrusting inside me. He pulled out of me as soon as he saw me open my eyes with a look of total shock and panic, and as I lay there unable to move, he jumped out of the tub and ran for the street while wrapping a beach towel around his waist.

I haven't shared what happened to me that night with anyone, until now, and though I never found out how many boys took advantage of me, I always felt like I deserved what happened. The humiliation of this tragedy, which propelled me further into a self-loathing coma, would take a couple of decades to emerge from. And while my shame wasn't overt, it always felt as heavy as a soaking wet wool coat that I could never take off.

Sadly, within a month I conjured up an idiotic plan with the hope of wiping my humiliated slate clean: I would use my first paycheck, from my first job, to throw a keg party with a live band at my house. The entrance fee was $1 per kid, but I have no memory of where the kegs came from, or where I found a band. My family had a trip to Knotts Berry Farm in Los Angeles planned for a weekend, and I lied about having to work. The reality, however, was that a couple of weeks into my job as a cashier at Lumber City I had been fired when $40 was discovered missing from my register. I hadn't taken it, but being perceived as a bad person and punished for a crime I didn't commit was a hard pill to swallow.

The keg party got out of control fast, so at about 11:00 pm I decided to call the police to break it up. When a couple of officers walked into the house, nearly one hundred high school kids ran out into the yard at once like scattering cockroaches.

With a tidal wave of destruction awaiting me in the morning, I had to spend my second (and last) paycheck, and the next forty-eight hours, shampooing carpets, cleaning up vomit and piss from the bathrooms, and repainting. The effort, however, was worth the feeling of redemption and of being perceived as cool—I hadn't been called a prick tease even once.

I started dating a scruffy boy I'd met at the party named Brian, who would take Toad, his scruffy pet goat, on a leash just about everywhere he went. It was nice to have a real boyfriend, and Toad acted like a dog. We had been dating for a couple of weeks when my father found me in bed with him—and in my father's bed, of all places—having fallen asleep after having sex. What the heck had I been thinking?

As my father roared into his bedroom with a twelve-inch butcher knife raised over his head shouting, "You better not be balling my daughter!" He swung the knife at Brian, who quickly darted out of the house, naked, pants in hand. Brian took off in his rose-colored Volkswagen van, with Toad in the back, never to be seen again.

After my father shamed me for about twenty minutes, he never again spoke of the incident.

I no longer recognized myself and surrendered to the exhaustion which resulted from manipulating boys into liking me and overcompensating in order to be included. If I had known there were kind and considerate boys out there, I may have held out for one, but I didn't know they existed, had never met any, and only knew boys who took advantage of girls. I vowed to take a break from boys and parties.

But that decision did not last long.

Go Ask Your Mother

The morning after I appeared in court, my father poked his head into my bedroom and nonchalantly said, "The sheriff was just here. You don't have to worry about that boy anymore, he was found dead in his bedroom."

My friend Amy and I were met by a thick wall of humidity from all the sweaty teenage bodies dancing ecstatically to *Rebel Rebel* by David Bowie. Although not officially invited to the party at the sprawling ranch house surrounded by acres of citrus orchards, we hoped if we walked in with confidence we'd be perceived as cool enough to be there.

Before Amy jumped into the dancing crowd she shouted, "Mary, you look foxy!"

Having borrowed her denim wrap around skirt and white tube top, I did feel foxy! But not being brave enough to jump into the middle of that mosh pit of about eighty drunk kids having a blast by making complete fools of themselves, went searching for some liquid courage instead.

After winding my way through the crowd I found the kitchen, where I spent a couple of hours drinking cheap beer with rowdy athletic types. When I was simultaneously sprayed with beer and a cheerleader vomited on the borrowed skirt, it was time to go. I couldn't find Amy in the house, so I went out to the driveway looking for her, as it was nearly midnight and her brother was supposed to pick us up any minute. When I was intercepted by a boy who had already graduated from high school, I described Amy and asked if he had seen her. Without saying a word, after staring at me for just a moment, he lurched toward me and flipped me over his shoulder. Reeking of wood and leather, most likely his father's cologne, he carried me into the orchard, running the entire way. I laughed for the first few jostling steps, until his shoulder started digging into my stomach, with my giggles quickly turning into screams when some low branches from several orange trees clawed at my back and ripped Amy's tube top off.

The young man threw me down onto the hard ground, and I landed flat on my back with a thud, losing my wind. As he jumped on top of me I grappled for air, the stench of his stale beer breath punching me in the face as he fumbled with the zipper on his jeans with one hand and ripped off my panties with the other.

Without the emotional will power to fight, he entered me. I didn't want to make him mad, thinking he would harm me. I laid there paralyzed because I didn't know what to do—I had no communication skills, or enough self-confidence, to deal with a situation like this. And I certainly didn't want to be called a prick tease again.

He didn't ask my name. He didn't say a word to me. He didn't want me for anything other than a female body to violate.

After rolling off me, he ran for a van that was idling in the driveway as his buddies called out his last name. I stood there in the dark orchard, paralyzed in shame, again. Topless, with blood dripping down the backs of my legs as my white ankle socks turned red, I couldn't find my shoes, my panties, or Amy's tube top, in the almost pitch black.

Amy was long gone by the time I emerged from the orchard. I didn't want anyone to see me half naked, and don't remember how I got to a phone booth to call my mother. My parents had recently separated, and she was temporarily living on my father's little sailboat at a marina about thirty-minutes away where she stayed after returning from her trip to Hawaii with Bob, the man she left our family for. She arrived in a little red sportscar, gave me her sweater, and took me to the emergency room.

With "rape kit" in hand, the emotionless ER doctor had to "get a sample of evidence" that might be lingering between my legs. I felt humiliated as he slowly plucked out a bunch of pubic hair, then plunged into my vagina with a large swab which he placed in a

That boy's actions and consequences fertilized a seed of shame in me that grew into a barbed vine around my heart which would define how I showed up in the world in relationships for decades to come.

---

test tube. He was grinding his teeth during the entire process while the police stood by waiting to take a statement from me.

As my mother drove me home from the emergency room at about 3:00 am she said, "I didn't really believe you until I saw the gashes on your back." Too traumatized and embarrassed to respond to her comment, I said nothing. In bed that night, I thought about why she would think I would make something like this up, and what I would possibly have to gain from going to the emergency room if I wasn't really hurt?

My father insisted we press charges. After I identified the twenty-year-old rapist by his last name and yearbook picture, he was arrested and put in jail, but it wasn't until thirty years later that I learned my father was able to visit him there the night before our court appearance. Always fierce for his daughters, I can only imagine what my father said to him.

On the day of my court appearance, after being told to wear something conservative, I sat in the rigid wooden box of a chair next to the judge looking like I belonged on the set of *Little House on the Prairie*. I felt nauseous as I pointed at the rapist and testified my truth of that awful evening in front of an audience that included my father. When the rapist's turn came to speak, he said I had suggested we go into the orchard to have sex, and I burst into silent tears as I ran out of the court room. I'm not sure what happened after I left, but knew he was allowed to go home with his mother that day. It wasn't until later that I learned his mother was the hall monitor who caught me smoking in the girl's bathroom in middle school, and had me kicked off the drill team.

The morning after I appeared in court, my father poked his head into my bedroom and nonchalantly said, "The sheriff was just here. You don't have to worry about that boy anymore, he was found dead in his bedroom."

The rapist was dead, my mother and father were relieved, but I was shocked. Did he take his own life? Did his father kill him? Did mine? I felt more grief for his mother than I did for his short life ending however it had. Although my parents never spoke of it again, I've thought about it over a million times.

After that, the world felt unsafe, and I no longer trusted anybody— not even myself. I felt responsible for what had happened, and unworthy of any relationship.

I dropped my social life, feeling extremely guilty for all the disastrous consequences of my careless choices. That boy's actions and consequences fertilized a seed of shame in me that grew into a barbed vine around my heart which would define how I showed up in the world in relationships for decades to come.

My rape story ultimately turned into a pity card I'd whip out of my back pocket whenever I needed a hit of sympathy. Because some men thrive on trying to save women from their misery, I attracted unstable knights in dull armor, and others who were equally as wounded as I who I felt the need to mother and take care of.

In my early forties, as I started speaking about my feelings of self-loathing around this rape experience with women I trusted, the abrasive grip of my shame finally began to loosen. But I didn't fully untangle its grip until decades later when I was able to receive the unconditional love of a healthy, happy, good-natured man who I share all of my stories with. And while he may flinch, this wonderful man feels no pity, with his love only deepening as he gets to know the story of my life. But more about Grant later.

In my early forties, as I started speaking about my feelings of self-loathing around this rape experience with women I trusted, the abrasive grip of my shame finally began to loosen.

It Was A Boy

It sounded like a torture chamber, and although my first thought was to scream at everyone to shut up, I was determined to be a compliant patient and not cause any trouble—or to upset my mother in any way.

Drops of opalescent liquid leaked out of my seventeen-year-old breasts through the knots of my crocheted halter top and onto the deck of my father's sailboat.

Praying no one would notice, I rubbed the drops of mystery fluid into the wood with my bare foot as I crossed my arms tightly over my chest. Shuffling up to the bow and sitting down with my back to everyone as we sailed around, jumping in the water, swimming back to the marina, and calling a girlfriend was all I wanted to do. This beautiful June day in 1977 was now ruined by the fear of what might be happening to me.

Panicked by the thought of having a fatal disease because something in my body had liquified and was coming out through my nipples, I went to the community health center the next day.

I was over twenty weeks pregnant, but didn't know it.

Sure, my breasts were getting fuller, my waist was thickening, and I had stopped having periods, but I didn't know this *wasn't* normal. In fact, I felt lucky I wasn't menstruating. I'd never had any talks with my parents about birth control, or the risk of pregnancy, so getting pregnant never even occurred to me.

The stoic nurse at the health center, who told me I had no choice but to have the baby, rambled on about "programs," then looked up from her clipboard with pencil in hand and asked me about the father. Not sure how to say that the father could have been one of three or more boys—some of whom were rapists—I gulped before saying, "I don't know."

Within a week my mother and father, who were in the throes of a messy divorce, found enough civility to drive me down to a clinic in Los Angeles that "took care of such things." Although grappling with the fear of what was about to happen, feeling a strange pleasure in seeing my mother and father together caused me to make a special effort to be on my best

behavior, so my only expression was one of quiet compliance. I didn't want to cause any more trouble for them, and believed that I was one of the problems that had caused the breakup of their marriage.

Our destination was in an industrial part of Los Angeles. Once in the nondescript concrete building, we were ushered to an old, peeling Formica table in a very bright room to sign a document. After being given a chewed-on Bic pen, and asked to write, "I am consenting to this procedure of my own free will," I felt my mother standing behind me and leaning into my upper body as if to ensure my completion of the task. Smelling like Aquanet hair spray, and something fermented, she was literally on my back, pushing my face to about ten inches from the paper as I slowly wrote out the statement in perfect cursive penmanship. As soon as I had signed my name, she quickly grabbed the pen and signed the paper as well, handed the man a check for $500, then lit a Pall Mall non-filtered cigarette—which I really wanted a hit of.

I was soon taken to a large cinderblock room with eleven other teenage girls who were all there for the same grim reason. With our hospital beds barely a few feet apart, separated only by plastic curtains, each of us was given an enema by a tired looking nurse, and told to hold it in until instructed, I barely made it to the bathroom when it was my turn. The girls who didn't make it were cursed by the tired ladies under their breath as they cleaned up after those who "messed" the floors.

Following the enema, I was brought into a room where a nervous man in a white coat inserted a long needle into my belly in order to replace the amniotic fluid with saltwater. After the procedure was over, he quietly said he was sorry and taped a piece of gauze where the needle had been. When I walked back to the cinderblock room it felt like a death march.

There was nowhere for my grief to go as my eyes darted around the little curtained-off world, looking for a place to put it. Wondering how anyone could ever love me after what I'd done— and what I'd let other people do to me.

After a few hours I joined the other eleven girls who were already in labor. While some sobbed silently, most of them were screaming in emotional and physical pain because they did not understand what was happening. It sounded like a torture chamber, and although my first thought was to scream at everyone to *shut up*, I was determined to be a compliant patient and not cause any trouble— or to upset my mother in any way. Thinking about all the other teenage girls who had labored in that bed before me, I whimpered in a fetal position throughout the night while enduring the relentless cramping in my belly.

My baby was born dead at 9:30 am the next morning, under the covers, unwitnessed, with no one to welcome it into the world. I apologetically called for a nurse, who came to my bedside to scoop up "the remains." As she whipped down the blanket, exposing a "stinky mess," I felt embarrassed for having soiled the sheets, but upon hearing the thud of a little body landing in the cold metal basin that she held over my abdomen, a molten mix of shame, humiliation, and guilt seared a permanent hole in my heart.

Just as the nurse was tossing the curtains aside to leave, she stopped, looked down in the basin, locked eyes with me, and with a flat affect said, "It was a boy."

There was nowhere for my grief to go as my eyes darted around the little curtained-off world, looking for a place to put it. Wondering how anyone could ever love me after what I'd done—and what I'd let other people do to me—I needed my mother to come and stroke my hair, to tell me I was brave, and that everything would be OK.

But it was my father's girlfriend who appeared at my beside instead. As Iris the Bitch grabbed the bloody sheet that was covering my legs, trying to pull it off to be sure the deed had been done, there was a brief tug-of-war, and she lost. Without a word she reached into her faux leather handbag, pulled out a Virginia Slim cigarette, and without taking her eyes off me put it in her mouth, lit it, then walked away.

Within minutes, another nurse came in and put something in my IV that immediately made me lightheaded—a feeling I welcomed gladly. She then unlocked the wheels of my blood-soaked bed and wheeled me in slow motion down an echoey hall under what seemed to be hundreds of brightly flickering fluorescent lights.

We arrived in a very cold room that contained two noose-like stirrups which appeared to be hanging from the ceiling. An empty soda can and a candy wrapper were on the floor at the feet of an expressionless man who wore blue coveralls and black rubber shoes. After receiving more medicine in my IV, or maybe in the plastic mask that was put over my nose and mouth, I drifted off to sleep as the nurse put my legs in the stirrups so they could vacuum out any remaining contents of my uterus before sending me home.

Upon leaving the procedure room, I was instructed to bind my breasts to prevent them from filling with milk, although I was too groggy to ask what that meant. What I really needed was assurance that I would be OK.

A gooey feminine pad the size of a brick shifted between my legs when I got into the backseat of my father's car. As we left the clinic with Tijuana Brass playing on the radio, I fell asleep hearing my parents talking about how the experience had been a nightmare for them. Although I had done something that made my mother happy, I had also done something I could not be forgiven for. We never spoke of the experience again.

I avoided thinking about my guilt and shame by continuing to engage in a chaotic teenage lifestyle, attempting to self-medicate with more alcohol and drugs in order to eliminate my pain. My anger toward my mother for such a complete lack of guidance and support soon grew into blaming her for everything that went wrong in my life.

If I had brought the child who I named Nathan Daniel into the world alive, he would be forty-five at the time of this writing. It was

only after years of inquiry that I learned my agreement to terminate the pregnancy had been motivated by my not wanting to make my mother mad, which would only push her further away from me. All I had wanted was for her to be proud of me—for something, anything—but at any expense. And I hated myself for this.

About twenty years later, with the experience haunting me enough to seek professional help, I was able to work through my emotional trauma with a therapeutic treatment called Eye Movement Desensitization Reprocessing (EMDR.) As a therapist guided me through reliving the trauma to the fullest extent possible, I simultaneously focused on the sound and feeling of my hands tapping my thighs and then snapping my fingers by my ears while looking side to side. The outcome felt miraculous, and although I still have memory of the traumatic event, the EMDR treatment was able to break the painful emotional symptoms I associated with it.

After unwinding the burden of my shame and guilt, which was then transformed into self-compassion, I was able to forgive myself. Since that time, I have also developed a greater understanding and compassion for the suffering other people experience due to choices they have made, a valuable skill I use regularly in my work as a hospice RN.

The Calling

In retrospect, I don't have any idea where I got the confidence to uproot and move 2500 miles away with only $600 in my pocket and no job.

Feeling a strong need to get as far away as I could from everybody who knew me, and my reputation, I decided to leave California. Little did I know, however, that my memories—and the person they had molded me into—would tag along.

Hawaii seemed like a good place to escape to.

The year before my move, I had visited the island of Oahu for a couple of weeks and stayed with my mother's sister, a frumpy lady who never had anything positive to say. Aunt Gayle, who was a hoarder, lived on a military base near Pearl Harbor, and I would borrow her decaying Nova almost every day to go into Waikiki to play on the sunny beaches. With the drinking age there eighteen, it felt like I'd won the partying lottery. Hanging out with loaded tourists was the most unrestricted I had felt in all of my eighteen years, and I really wanted that freedom back.

In retrospect, I don't have any idea where I got the confidence to uproot and move 2500 miles away with only $600 in my pocket and no job.

The long-awaited day came, and I awoke at 4:30 am in order to take a taxi to the Greyhound bus station as I had to be at LAX by 11:30 am to catch a flight to Honolulu. Once at the deserted station, I sat in the cold predawn light for about forty-five minutes with the irrational hope that my mother would be there to send me off with a hug or a kiss—she knew I was leaving on this day. I ended up getting on the bus without a send off, arriving in Honolulu an unremarkable ten hours later, greeted only by a sign that read Welcome to Paradise.

High on the smell of jet fuel and plumeria, after hopping on a city bus that took me to Waikiki, I stayed at a dumpy hotel for three weeks before finding a month-to-month, cockroach infested, shared apartment that I'd learned about from a newspaper ad.

As fate would have it, my two roommates were twenty-something party girls with benefits. After spending two weeks getting to know their circle of seemingly wealthy friends, dancing all night buzzing on expensive drinks and snorting unlimited supplies of cocaine, I really did feel free. My new friends paid for boating adventures, expensive meals, and picked up the tab at fancy beach bars— I had hit the jackpot of fun.

Having just quit my job as a legal secretary in California, it was easy to get work at a law firm in Honolulu. Although I soon found the nine to five lifestyle a near impossible adjustment to make—it cramped my ability to stay up late partying and sleeping in until noon—it turned out to be a beneficial change of pace. When my roommate's rich friends moved to Maui, I learned the reason they could afford all the cocaine and good times was because they were stealing wallets out of unattended purses on Waikiki Beach. After taping off the signature line of a stolen credit card, covering the owner's signature with paint and signing their own names, they'd get cash advances and go on two-hour shopping sprees before destroying the card. Eventually, they were arrested for it, and I could have been in the middle of it—but that nine to five had spared me.

I soon met a charismatic party animal at a disco one Friday after work who approached me as a male equivalent of a damsel in distress by coming on all lonely and needy. But when he invited me to go waterskiing on his speedboat, I joyfully accepted the invitation.

After being picked up in a fancy black and gold 280ZX, I felt like a queen while driving with the top down along the beautiful turquoise coastline of Oahu with my new friend—a thirty-two-year old former used car salesman from Montana who had become a cocaine dealer in Hawaii. After a couple of glorious adventure dates, he invited me to quit my job at the law firm and move in with him on a cockroach-free beach front property he rented in Hawaii Kai, about ten miles from Waikiki. Since he was equipped to support the lifestyle I longed for, I carelessly said yes. Although he informed me soon after I moved in that I was a *decoration* with an expiration date, I was willing to be his arm candy for free rent, free food, and as much cocaine as I wanted.

He grew tired of me in about ten months, and gave me the boot—along with gonorrhea—so his new decoration could take my place. No blood was shed in this breakup, and I never did cocaine again.

It was easy to find an apartment in town that needed another roommate, and I strung together odd jobs to pay the rent so I could still play on the beach. I was confident of molding myself into any environment, and doing just fine, although upon reflection I'm not sure if I was a confident risk taker, or just ignorant of what could go wrong.

One day, while taking a break from the sun in front of the shaded Surfrider Hotel in Waikiki, I was tapped on the shoulder by a police officer, who then handcuffed me. This arrest had been for solicitation on a busy stretch of Waikiki beach, and without the story behind it—which you will soon hear—it is often perceived as prostitution.

Wearing only a bikini, I was escorted by the elbow along a beach access path between two major hotels, down a sidewalk on a busy avenue, then put in the back of a squad car that smelled like booze and body odor. During my walk of shame several tourists lifted their cameras from their necks to capture the busty blond in a neon green string bikini in handcuffs. Humiliated, I hung my head and covered my face with my hair like people do on cop shows who are getting arrested in public. To make matters worse, my bikini top needed constant adjusting, but the handcuffs didn't allow me to make the necessary adjustments to the little pieces of triangular fabric, so when my nipples started migrating toward freedom, there was nothing I could do about it.

After arriving at the police station, I posed for a mugshot taken by a smirky police officer who told me to smile at the camera, so I found a crooked one for him. Someone tossed me a large, stained Budweiser t-shirt to wear as I walked into a holding cell filled with unsavory and intoxicated characters who looked at me like I was a hot fudge sundae with a neon sign over my head that said *eat me.*

I tried not to stare at an anxious woman cowering in the corner on the floor, and while exuding the vibe of a tough chick and repeating *nobody look at me, nobody talk to me* over and over in my head, waited nervously to be bailed out by Rocco, my employer—and boyfriend.

THE CALLING | 61

Rocco was a pudgy, pipe-smoking man in his early thirties with a thick gold chain around his neck and a gap between his stained front teeth.

I had met Rocco a year prior when he approached me with an odd question at the beach in front of The Royal Hawaiian Hotel as I was toweling off after a swim.

"Are you a medium?"

As I reapplied sunscreen to my arms, my answer included a question of my own.

"I guess so, why?"

It turned out he was starting up Bikini Goddess Swimwear, a bikini manufacturing business, and needed a model for his size medium. He didn't have the vibe of a bikini designer, his personality was more like a pawn shop manager, but when I met him at his studio the following weekend his seamstress quickly took my measurements, then proceeded to sew some well fitted tops and bottoms for me.

Rocco asked me out on a real date and took me to La Mer, a very expensive restaurant in Waikiki in an upscale hotel called the Halekulani. Although now twenty-one, I had never had food that good before, and really felt special. But when I didn't agree to have sex with Rocco that night, he made me feel like I owed it to him because of the expensive dinner. The next night he took me to another fancy restaurant, Nick's Fishmarket.

My perfect job at Bikini Goddess Swimwear was to slowly walk along the two mile stretch of Waikiki Beach wearing a designer bikini in search of women who looked like they may value a custom made two-piece. I toted professional photographs of me wearing a variety of bikinis, along with fabric swatches and sample suits potential customers could try on over their own. I also carried a clunky walkie-talkie for calling in orders, so the seamstresses could start sewing immediately. I would make deliveries to hotel rooms that same evening with a small hand gun strapped to my ankle, just in case I got into trouble in the room—which was Rocco's idea. I didn't know how to shoot the thing, or even get it out of its holster, but for some reason felt protected.

Before long, I moved in with Rocco on the twenty-fourth floor of a magnificent high rise condominium in Waikiki. I felt classy living there, and though we soon became lovers, it was more like he masturbated inside of me like a clammy jack hammer. He would often tell me I didn't know how to please a man, but the noises he made while we were having sex would indicate otherwise, because he sounded like a happy pig.

If the internet had been invented back then, I would have searched, "How to please a man," but it was a girlfriend who told me to give him a blowjob, instructing me how to suck, not blow, on his dick. When I first tried it, making gagging sounds like a choking seal until he ejaculated on my relieved face, it was awful. After that, he wanted a blow job just about every night. Pleasing him felt like my duty because I wasn't paying for rent or food, but it was a repulsive way to live.

Once, when he asked me to cook dinner for him and a couple of friends, and I proudly boiled some pasta, cooked ground beef, and added a jar of Ragu spaghetti sauce, Rocco said he couldn't serve it. After dumping it in the trash, he ordered takeout from an expensive Japanese restaurant down the street just as his snobby friends came over. When they questioned why there wasn't a homemade meal as promised, and Rocco said, "Oh, I didn't realize that Mary can't cook," I felt painfully inadequate. Although fifteen years later I would become a personal chef and film cooking segments for television in my own gourmet kitchen, when cooking for Rocco and his friends, I had not yet achieved any culinary artistry.

It certainly seemed I couldn't do much right for this man, except sell his bikinis and open my legs and mouth for him. I felt like an object, and knew he didn't value me as a person, so I began asking myself what it was I valued myself for.

Able to at least acknowledge my skill at being mostly comfortable around people I didn't know, peddling bikinis, and saving money, I also appreciated that I was getting exercise *and* a tan while earning a commission of $3.60 per suit—which added up to $80 in tax-free cash per day, a lot of money in 1981.

Which brings us back to my being arrested.

The beaches in front of each hotel in Waikiki were monitored by a nearly invisible presence of local men who called themselves The Beach Boys—a mafia of sorts who protected their sandy acreage from others. After about two months of dealing bikinis, they wanted me to give them a cut of my profits for doing business in front of "their" hotels. Because my answer was no, they called the

THE CALLING | 63

police and had me arrested for solicitation.

My job at Bikini Goddess Swimwear ended that day Rocco brought $50 to the police station to spring me out of jail. When I took off the borrowed t-shirt, and he told me I was getting fat (at all of 118 pounds on a 5' 8" frame), I realized how much I hated his insulting company. Being quite tired of being his mediocre sex slave, and bad cook as well, it was the perfect time to leave him.

I soon moved in with a wholesome, maternal fifty-year-old woman who sold encyclopedias door to door, a good move for my impressionable character. With only a bike for transportation, the ride up the steep two-mile hill we lived on in St. Louis Heights above the University of Hawaii was handy for staying in shape.

I took another job soliciting, this time pressuring men into buying their dates roses and leis. Cruising through Waikiki restaurants with a basket of flowers while wearing a skin-tight taffeta dress with poofy sleeves and high heels, after locking eyes with a man who was dining with a woman, I'd smile ever so sweetly and ask if he'd like to buy his beautiful date some flowers.

If his answer was no, his date might think he didn't think she was beautiful, so my shameless tactic worked 90% of the time. I received a commission for each flower sold, and my daily stops at ten restaurants, a couple of discos, a super fun gay bar called Dirty Mary's, and a wild strip club called the Lollipop earned me $90— twice that on military paydays. I'd often receive free drinks as well, and sometimes food.

When I needed a little extra money I'd enter, and typically win, bikini contests for a $200 prize at The Shorebird, a beach bar on Waikiki.

I loved this lifestyle because it allowed me to play on the beach all day, but I was always just barely able to pay my rent.

I found a second job as a cocktail waitress at Bobby McGee's restaurant and disco, where I changed my name to Ruby, wore a tuxedo jacket with tails over a white dress shirt with a red bow tie and matching cummerbund, under which I wore fishnet stockings, high heels, and a little black panty. Ruby soon developed a habit of calmly spilling drinks on ballsy men who ventured to pat her rear or lift up the tails on her tuxedo jacket to check out her back side—I sure loved it when the drink on my tray at the time of such an infraction was a glass of red wine. After having developed the knack of keeping my cool in the pandemonium of a roaring disco, staying calm in chaotic situations is a quality I continue to carry with me.

While selling flowers to the wealthy tourists and movie stars who dined at Nick's Fishmarket— that high end restaurant the snobby bikini maker had taken me to—I met a busboy who invited me to a party he was throwing.

Upon arriving at his house, I found him tending bar in his living room while wearing powder blue overalls without a shirt underneath. His tanned shoulder muscles were impressive, and he smelled like something deliciously reminiscent of Thanksgiving at my grandmother's—which turned out to be the Right Guard deodorant he sprayed on his clothes instead of washing them. But his bleached blond hair from playing in the sun made up for that, and he was definitely my type. Although I found it odd that he didn't pay much attention to me while I was in his home, I soon understood that he was a silent, moody type who loved to smoke weed and party hard.

Despite those first impressions, I said yes to muddy jungle hikes, beach dates at sunset with gourmet goodies, and exhilarating sailing adventures on a huge trimaran with one of his salty dog sailor friends. After he moved up the ladder at Nick's—from busboy to waiter to sommelier—with access to limousines, and familiarity with all the waitstaff at the best restaurants in town, we would go out often. This was when I learned to appreciate fine dining and good wine, and he taught me the basics of gourmet cooking, which I blossomed from and continue to nurture.

We had been together for five years when we spent some time exploring Europe, which included a bicycle and wine tour in the Burgundy region of France. We picked out a little diamond ring in Belgium, and he proposed to me two weeks later in the south of France. My answer was yes.

I began taking classes at Kapiolani Community College, started running again, and soon transferred to the University of Hawaii at Manoa to pursue a degree in biomedical sciences. Cracked opened to a part of me that thrived with learning about the human body, I took every human anatomy and physiology class I could. Spending time with all those smart, healthy athletic types ultimately inspired me to train for a marathon.

I broke the engagement off when I could no longer relate to his marijuana use, drinking habits, worsening irritability, and anger. Every night after work he'd come home high, with an awful fermented breath I could barely tolerate, and was often too hungover to participate in the fun activities we used to enjoy.

Within a year of our separation, my former fiancé was given the opportunity to sail a sleek racing sailboat from Oahu to California. Somewhere in the middle of the journey while keeping a solo watch during a storm at sunset, he was swept overboard into the churning sea, unwitnessed. Although almost an hour had passed before he was discovered missing, the crew circled around with a rope towing a life preserver in hopes of snagging him. While in the water, upon losing sight of the boat he promised God to stop drinking and smoking marijuana if given another chance at life. He also made a vow to God he would marry me clean and sober, and be a good father to our unborn children. I was unconvinced, but he was persistent, and within a year, when my father died suddenly, it was I who proposed that we get married right away—which we did. At the time, I didn't understand the suddenness of my decision, but in retrospect, it felt like a rebound to the death of my father because we were married within a month of his passing.

Over the next four years we had two daughters, lived in a little cottage in his mother's backyard, and both attended school while working at restaurants. I'd sometimes come home to find his mother—a large, German evangelical Christian who pushed all my buttons—who had my preschool aged daughters kneeling in front of a booming television watching evangelical events while keeping a firm grip on each of their heads and speaking in tongues. I didn't have the communication skills to tell her how I felt about her actions, and feared making her angry, but more than once told her she had a fly on her cheek so she would smack herself in the face.

My husband became moodier and more irritable, and I later learned his bursts of rage and lecturing aimed at me and our daughters was not about us, but about his needs not being met when he was a child. Only once did he slap our older daughter, and when he did I pushed him through the screen door of our cottage. After he landed on his ass on the concrete, I roared at him with my whole body to *never* touch her like that again.

Although I wanted to leave him, I couldn't afford to (yet), but was able to find healthy ways to redirect my frustration about our marriage, and my anger about my childhood, with swimming, biking, running, and competing in triathlons.

At the time, I didn't understand the suddenness of my decision, but in retrospect, it felt like a rebound to the death of my father because we were married within a month of his passing.

Me Too

Keeping my eyes on the road while clipping along at twenty miles an hour, although the other traffic was speeding up, the blue Toyota maintained its pace with me which enabled the drunk boy in the front passenger seat to lean out the window just far enough to reach me.

During a euphoric ride on my turquoise green Bianchi road bike, flying down Kalaniana'ole Highway on the island of Oahu I couldn't tell if my tires were actually touching the road. Feeling high on life, invincible, and incredibly grateful for my strong athletic body, I was testing out a new black and red one piece *tri suit* that looked like one of those conservative onesie bathing suits women wore in the 1920s, and which was remarkably comfortable to swim, bike, and run in. As I kept pace with traffic on parts of that fantastic stretch of highway, the wind at my back, I was heading for Kapiolani Park and the finish line to the half Ironman I was training for.

Thriving in triathlon and marathon competition, as well as university lifestyle, I was the happiest I'd been in years. Nothing pleased me more than studying on the beach after runs, long bike rides, and swims. This was before marriage and children when I was in school full time, had a glorious training schedule, and worked as a cocktail waitress in a hopping disco at night. At twenty-four, life was grand.

Near the end of my magnificent twenty-five-mile ride along that breathtaking stretch of Hawaiian coastline, I noticed a blue compact Toyota along side of me and could hear (and feel) *Burning Down the House* by the Talking Heads blaring through its closed windows. Four boisterous boys in the car were laughing and carrying on as cans of Budweiser beer sloshed all over them.

My first thought was the hope that they would make it to wherever they were going without hurting themselves, or other people. But as one of boys in the back seat rolled his window down and shouted "Hey baby, want to sit on my face?" and the other three laughed hysterically, I let out a huff of disgust. Keeping my eyes on the road while clipping along at twenty miles an hour, although the other traffic was speeding up, the blue Toyota maintained its

pace with me which enabled the drunk boy in the front passenger seat to lean out the window just far enough to reach me. As the others in the car cheered on this floundering boy, the driver swerved into the bike lane and took his right hand off the steering wheel in order to hold onto the idiot boy's left leg so he wouldn't fall out of the car. The idiot then grabbed my breasts with both hands, squeezed them hard, and refused to let go as the other boys ramped up their drunken shouts of approval.

Sobbing, and making unrecognizable sounds, I stopped pedaling but continued to be pulled along by the moving car. As I gripped the handlebars with all my might, and avoided crashing by not braking, I had to endure being dragged by my breasts as other cars whizzed by.

When the boy decided it was over, and finally let go, I screamed and cursed while he and his friends shrieked with laughter as their car sped ahead, swerving almost out of control. After hitting the brakes so hard I almost toppled over the front of my bike, I was able to make out the license plate number through tears of rage and humiliation.

I managed to call the police from a telephone booth at a gas station across the street— incomprehensible, even to myself, and so nauseated I thought I would throw up on my new biking shoes. When a beefy police officer arrived after twenty minutes I had just stopped shaking violently— freezing cold despite standing in the warm Hawaiian sun. Speaking to me in a condescending voice as if I was a helpless airhead, he said the car was a rental, the boys were tourists, and it would be difficult to track them down.

After I made one final complaint, the police officer said something that changed my life forever as he slowly looked me up and down, gazed at my chest, and spoke directly to my breasts: "What did you expect, look at what you are wearing."

The police officer said something that changed my life forever as he slowly looked me up and down, gazed at my chest, and spoke directly to my breasts: "What did you expect, look at what you are wearing."

Feeling totally violated, again, my shoulders hunched forward as my chest caved into my body—a position in which it would remain in for many years to come. Was he right that I deserved it? *Was it my fault?* I felt shame both for what he said, and for not speaking up for myself. I don't remember what happened next, but somehow got myself back onto my bike and rode home.

It was only recently that I heard a reflection on this story from a friend that I wish I could have received back then: "Your courage and instincts to stop pedaling and go with it for your safety was a fierce act of self-love." But because I didn't hear that from anyone all those years ago, it felt like my body only attracted trouble—and that men were not to be trusted.

To this day, I am uncomfortable wearing tight clothing in public, and don't want to draw unwanted attention to myself, especially my breasts. And while many men have told me to flaunt it while I've got it, instead, I tend to dress more like a librarian.

Although I slowly unlearned the devastating effects of this experience by eventually surrounding myself with people, including men, who actually value and appreciate women, it took decades to find myself in such a crowd.

Now, with the creation of this book, I'm letting every bit of me be seen.

Murmuration

Without any coping tools or defenses available, I absorbed every inch of their pain until my bones ached. Feeling changed forever, I grieved for something I couldn't name.

With a goal of becoming a doctor, and more credits than needed to graduate from the University of Hawaii with an undergraduate degree in biomedical sciences, when the opportunity to shadow doctors for two weeks at The Queens Medical Center in Honolulu came up, I jumped at the chance.

My first day included a grueling and unprecedented morning in the emergency room where I witnessed the horrible physical and emotional pain of a fifty-year-old woman who had been beaten by her husband with a baseball bat. Standing stunned and paralyzed in the doorway of the trauma room, seeing how her enormous physical and emotional distress was causing this badly injured woman to want to die, I felt her pain deep in my gut—even though I had never been physically harmed like that.

The ER doctor looked at me with surprising composure as he silently pointed to the spot where I was to stand and observe. Unable to focus on anything but a black scuff mark on the wall next to me, I couldn't exhale, and knew if I made eye contact with the tormented woman I would lose all self-control, perhaps even soiling my pants.

Grateful to be called out of the trauma room to watch a nurse treating a homeless person with tooth pain who seemed to be experiencing moderate discomfort, my heart sank for this man who was being accused of drug seeking, and thus treated very poorly.

An hour later, a commotion in the ER staff preceded the presentation of a teenage boy who had been hit by a car, then pronounced dead on arrival. When his mother arrived, she collapsed on the floor and thrashed around while wailing inconsolably, and I realized I had never witnessed a grief which penetrated my very being like this woman's did.

Not prepared to bear witness to such intense expressions of suffering, I felt overwhelmingly helpless and hyperventilated as the room began to spin. Without any coping tools or defenses available, I absorbed every inch of their pain until my bones ached. Feeling changed forever, I grieved for something I couldn't name.

When the ER doctor said I looked a little pale and asked if I was okay, I stared at him blankly before hurrying to the nearest trash can to vomit. Seeing the suffering of others felt like too much to handle, and I realized I couldn't stand to be in that environment for another minute. I calmly and politely excused myself, and then ran to my car, where I cried hysterically in the parking lot. Even though I never went back, that experience was just what was needed to save my own life.

In a few years I would learn why I had reacted the way I did in the ER: I hadn't recognized, or embraced, my own suffering, so how could I compassionately embrace anyone else's? My own trauma was rotting somewhere in my gut, and having never allowed myself to feel it, I was deeply triggered in the presence of great pain and suffering.

Quickly changing my biomedical science major to exercise science, I went on to become an athletic trainer. Helping motivated athletes recover from their injuries felt safer than medicine, and for a few years I flew under the radar from any substantial suffering by working for physical therapists, as well as with clients of my own as a personal trainer. I eventually returned to school to earn a Master's degree in public health, where I happily made great strides in learning how to make a difference in the health and wellbeing of my community.

Then, when it was time to choose a thesis topic, I was put on a lifesaving path to personal inquiry, unlearning, and the healing of my childhood wounding.

I hadn't recognized, or embraced, my own suffering, so how could I compassionately embrace anyone else's?

The Myth of Me

My goal was to see how my presentation of symptoms would be perceived, diagnosed, and treated across a spectrum of multicultural, physical, social, psychological, holistic, and spiritual healing traditions.

Playing a silent game of peek-a-boo with a little girl perched on her mother's shoulder while waiting in line for a bagel in the food court at the mall, I was as happy as could be. Graduate school was starting in a couple weeks, and I was fueling up to buy clothes that serious grad students wore.

But just as I took a step forward in line, my heart began pounding and the sound of blood swooshing in my ears became louder and louder. It had suddenly become stifling hot, and as sweat dripped down my spine, an alarming tickle progressed in my throat to the point where I couldn't breathe without conscious effort. I feared I might faint right there on the spot.

Looking around to see if other people were also noticing the walls closing in, I didn't catch any displays of impending doom on anyone else's face or in their body language—except for my own—they were all just going about their business. But as my hands began to tremble with unbearable panic and I dropped my wallet, I knew it was time to find an exit.

These attacks, which had been coming on more frequently, were accompanied by muscle spasms in my neck and back that might seize me for a few hours, or put me to bed for days. I didn't know it at the time, but suppression of unresolved childhood trauma was catching up with me and bubbling up as crippling fibromyalgia, anxiety, and panic. Having been prescribed pain killers, muscle relaxants, and sedatives (which were only partially effective), finding a functional balance between feeling loopy and aware enough to go about my day at school and at home was essential. Even so, I was barely able to take care of two children under five while doing my best to sustain a marriage that was not serving my heart or soul.

When it came time to pick a thesis topic, I decided to do research on myself in hopes of understanding the origins of my physical and emotional pain. I

sought counsel from a wide variety of practitioners—from traditional western to nontraditional eastern medicine, shamanic to celestial guidance, as well as a few other-worldly interventionalists—and visited as many of these specialists as possible in the eighteen months provided to complete the project. After asking all thirty something of them the same question, *What's wrong with me*, I collected thirty diagnoses, and braved most of their treatments.

My goal was to see how my presentation of symptoms would be perceived, diagnosed, and treated across a spectrum of multi-cultural, physical, social, psychological, holistic, and spiritual healing traditions, and I didn't see the practitioners in any particular order. After starting with my allopathic health provider, I merely went with the flow of who was presented to me to consult with next.

After my medical doctor recommended a psychiatrist who prescribed an antidepressant and two different sedatives, and feeling numb from those medications (almost like I couldn't fully experience joy), I was sent to a psychologist who lured me into a talk therapy group for young moms where I was told *I am not my thoughts*. But after being in a circle of stressed out moms where one woman admitted giving her kids Benadryl every afternoon so she could get her housework done and dinner started without interruption, and an assortment of other overwhelming mommy confessions too much to witness, I decided I didn't belong in that group.

After a friend recommended her homeopathic practitioner, whose little sugary beads dissolved under my tongue three times a day to help my body heal itself only made me crave raw chocolate chip cookie dough, the homeopath led me to her partner, a naturopath, who suggested limiting animal protein and removing all grains, sugar, dairy, and certain fruits and vegetables from my plate, which I did—and promptly lost fifteen pounds off an already thin frame. But I was always tired, and my hair and nails became brittle, at which point a nutritionist across the street was certain I just needed to eat *more* of all fruits and vegetables while paying special attention to what my poop looked and smelled like (I started pooping like a champion).

The nutritionist then recommended an osteopath, who manipulated my upper body and gave me a spongy cervical collar for my persistent neck pain—which I soon became reliant on, and felt unsafe without.

The osteopath sent me to his favorite massage therapist, who practiced Rolfing, and who set in to piss off the connective tissue in my back while using metal friction tools which left burn marks on my skin. Since I couldn't tolerate her painful treatments, the Rolfer dismissed me to a very relaxing Lomi Lomi therapist who lovingly massaged me with kuikui nut oil scented with Hawaiian flowers and placed warmed lava rocks along my spine—and whose kind touch I never wanted to leave.

The Lomi Lomi practitioner recommended a physical therapist she saw for her own back problems who found certain muscles in my neck were weak, and prescribed exercises with resistance bands and stretching.

The physical therapist then recommended a chiropractor, who found me to be out of alignment, so he cracked my joints and sent me to a surgeon to be evaluated for a possible herniated disc in my neck because I was a competitive road biker. When the surgeon offered to cut me, like surgeons do, I rode my bike away from his office rolling my eyes under my photochromic sunglasses which were recommended by an ophthalmologist because the glare on the road could have been overexerting my eye and facial muscles and contributing to tightness in my neck.

One of my teachers at school suggested I see her acupuncturist who put needles in my neck and ears, then suggested I see a Chinese herbalist, who found that my life force needed reinforcement and had me drinking herbal potions that tasted like the smell of compost. I held my nose and drank the special elixirs, and developed a sense of braveness and accomplishment for doing so.

An ayurvedic practitioner trained in India found deficiencies in my physical, emotional, and spiritual energies which she said left openings for disability, and offered ways to detoxify these parts of me with herbal formulas and by dripping medicated oil on my forehead during a massage.

In the center of a prayer circle with twelve hands on my body infusing me with God's healing light, I was unexpectedly brought to tears by the powerful feelings which arose. Years later, I gathered several of my dearest friends and used this same hopeful technique on my daughter before one of her cancer surgeries. I have a gut feeling this was a reason for her positive outcome.

I've experimented with hypnosis, relaxation therapies, guided imagery, muscle testing, meditation, Reiki, therapeutic touch, singing bowl therapy, and biofeedback. I've kept a negative ion plate in my back pocket, a water feature in my bedroom, Tibetan prayer flags over my front door, multiple crystals on an altar on my dresser, and bundles of sage in an abalone shell on my mantle to burn when my environment needs cleansing.

I learned about a psychic healer from the crystal shop where I bought a rose quartz bracelet to promote positive energy and self-love, but didn't buy into psychic healing right away as it all sounded too contrived. However, a few years after graduate school, I reluctantly met with a psychic healer who took me on a past life regression adventure that transformed this lifetime forever (the exciting story about this unbelievable experience is coming up).

After a shaman told me I was carrying pain and suffering from past lifetimes that manifested in physical and emotional pain, I didn't feel emotionally strong enough to bear witness or cope with what might be found by working with him further, and waited a few years before engaging in unimaginable ceremonies with a female shaman that I was surprised to find I resonated with.

Since that time, Shamans have interacted with the spirit worlds on my behalf on several occasions where I was gifted amazing shifts in perspectives and healing—on one of these occasions I danced, sweated, played drums, and rattled my intentions for healing around a fire in a tipi during a ceremony where I received the warrior name *Bright Day*.

A shaman channeled Mary Magdalena on my behalf with some revealing truths which cracked my heart wide open and helped make sense of the lifetimes I've lived so far.

There are three shamanic ceremonies that will be shared later in this book: In one, a part of my soul was brought back to me that fled during a traumatic childhood experience from another lifetime; in another, I was taken back in time to find the root cause of my negative self-image. Finally, a shaman channeled Mary Magdalena on my behalf with some revealing truths which cracked my heart wide open and helped make sense of the lifetimes I've lived so far.

What I learned from these inquiries during graduate school is that practitioners diagnose and suggest treatments based on their individual training, beliefs, and curiosities—and they all see the human body through their own personalized lenses. Some practitioners just see physical dysfunction or disease; others embrace the mind, body, spirit, community, and environmental connections to health and wellbeing.

This exploration, which extended ten years beyond graduation, helped me realize that I would not be able to help others who were suffering until I was able to help myself. I needed to heal my own life. My childhood wounds needed to be revealed, and loved, so I could move forward with the unlikely career choice which awaited me: Hospice.

PART TWO
Unlearning

Dreadlocks

With a coin toss, my young family planned a six-week summer trip to Oregon (over Washington, Idaho, or Colorado) in hopes of finding a beautiful, fair-weathered place to relocate to after I graduated with my master's degree in public health (MPH). Honolulu had become too expensive, too crowded, and the constant sun exposure was a moderate risk for me and my little towhead daughters.

Before leaving for Oregon, I had arranged to do an internship at Ashland Community Hospital in Southern Oregon. Lori, who was my clinical supervisor there, would become a lifelong mentor and cherished friend.

During this trip, an exciting employment opportunity as a cardiac rehabilitation educator became available at a different hospital in a neighboring town, so I confidently interviewed, quickly had a second interview, passed the required physical, and was hired. I was thrilled at the prospect of working with people who had survived heart attacks or open-heart surgeries and guiding them on paths to healthy recoveries.

It sounded like a dream job that would fit my desires and qualifications.

Upon graduating, I packed up my daughters, moved to Oregon, and my husband joined us in about a month as he was reluctant to leave his mother, who was in poor health. A week after arriving in Oregon, and signing a

yearlong lease on a house, I attended the new employee orientation only to be told I didn't qualify for the job after all—they had made a mistake.

The embarrassed and apologetic woman in human resources said the job requirements were an Oregon Registered Nurse license, and while an MPH was preferred, it was not required. They had never mentioned this in my interviews, and I was led to believe they meant either an RN license or an MPH was required. My master's focus had been community health education and cardiovascular disease prevention and control, so coupled with my biomedical sciences background, I thought I was a perfect fit—but my hard work and previous accomplishments were not good enough. Devastated about the miscommunication, I also took the rejection personally.

However, it was no mistake that I had been lured from Honolulu to Ashland, Oregon.

My new friend Lori brought me and my sad state of affairs to a small circle of big-hearted wise women who held a safe and loving space for me. Although Lori didn't say why she had brought me there, and I felt like I was just going along for the ride, this group became my forever beloved sisterhood and helped me unlearn thirty year's worth of lies I had chosen to believe.

But at our first meeting, when Mira, the gracious facilitator of the circle, asked a simple question that landed in the center of my thirty-eight-year-old chest like a stun gun, knocking the wind out of me, I spiraled into a slow panic and considered running for the door.

I had been asked, quite frankly, what I didn't like about myself.

Sharing my perceived faults and insecurities in front of other people, regardless of the safe environment, felt painfully vulnerable. Even an eye roll from any of these strong, capable women who actually loved

With the intensity of a thousand warriors, these gentle, compassionate women—Mira, Lori, and Geri—proceeded to love my self-loathing to death while breathing life into my conviction to heal.

---

themselves, each other, and me (for what reason I could not say) seemed more than I could bear. I feared that admission of my scariest truths would brand me as undeserving of membership in this group, but also felt unable to deceive myself any longer.

Mira pulled me from the hole I was digging for myself to hide in by asking if she could read something to me. Nodding yes, I took a noisy deep breath through flared nostrils, then slowly exhaled through trembling lips, grateful for the extra few moments before having to answer the question which would ultimately expose me. After asking me to keep my eyes on her, Mira slowly opened a notebook on her lap and began to read aloud:

"All of her life she had been told lies that she thought were the truth, how could she know the difference? Until a wise woman came along and saw a grain of truth and nurtured it until it was huge and powerful. That woman is you, Mary."

My heart broke open as I let out a primal scream that filled every inch of the room. Weeping without reservation, layer after layer of unresolved mother wounding became visible, until unable to outrun my pain anymore, the lies that I had been juggling and spinning like plates were allowed to come into full view. With the intensity of a thousand warriors, these gentle, compassionate women—Mira, Lori, and Geri—proceeded to love my self-loathing to death while breathing life into my conviction to heal.

This beloved sisterhood met me in all of my dark places, and held me up without ever dropping me. With their consistent loving support and witnessing, I was able to strip myself of years of expertly layered armor created to hide my true nature. Trusting in their unconditional love, I exposed the entirety of my wounded and raw self, in painful increments, over a period of about ten years. During this time, in spite of my becoming transparent and extremely vulnerable, their love for me never wavered.

Throughout my multi-decade journey with these incredible women, I learned that my low self-esteem and lack of confidence had locked me into a sense of worthlessness. Without parental direction as a child, I was locked in survival mode without boundaries, forced to learn lessons the hard way, often by humiliation; moreover, the absence of a nurturing mother had locked me into questioning my own value, to believe that love never lasts, and not to trust anyone. My childhood wounding had also taught me to live as a victim.

And my self-expression was locked under all the trauma I had experienced in my life, until now.

This beloved sisterhood offered me keys to begin unlocking, and unlearning, the lessons of the root causes of the pain which had caused so much misery as I emerged from a dysfunctional childhood. After sitting in their profoundly intimate circle for the past twenty-five years, I credit them for nurturing me onto a courageous path to my true glorious self—they have kept me on a heroic journey of self-discovery and healing to this day.

It was no mistake that I had been lured from Honolulu to Ashland, Oregon.

Higher Selves

She had found me in a past lifetime in the early 1800s. I was a thirty-three-year-old Chinese man wandering a war-torn countryside on horseback—wounded and starving.

Carly, a psychic healer, opened our telephone conversation in a soft spoken, matter of fact way, explaining that although she doesn't have healing powers, as a channel for the spirit world she's able to provide information from another plane of existence which can help heal unresolved physical pain.

I thought it felt absurd to meet over the phone, and almost asked if there would be any benefit from the session if I didn't believe in her abilities. But since the session had been gifted to me by my beloved friend Geri, and I really had nothing to lose, I launched into my story.

In one long exhale, I flippantly described the turmoil of my younger life, and its perceived effect on my present-day experiences. But as I began explaining my suffering from fibromyalgia, and the crippling anxiety and panic which accompanied it, she stopped my rant and asked curtly if I'd like to find out why I have these problems—and possibly find a solution to healing. At this, I sat straighter in my chair, swallowing hard at the thought of what it would be like to not be in pain as a surprising mist gathered in my eyes. When she asked if I would be willing to take steps for healing in an astral realm, my answer was emphatic. "I would do anything to make my pain go away."

The session began with a grounding exercise of breathing and relaxation, followed by a meeting of our higher selves on the astral plane, where we would tap into humanity's eternal library—the Akashic records.

Carly was then quiet for a few moments while I sat growing nervous at my kitchen table, wide eyed with anticipation of what was going to happen next. Palms down, I fumbled with crumbs from my kids' breakfast toast eaten an hour earlier before they left for school.

Soon, I could hear Carly making quiet sounds of agreement, as if receiving instructions. After another long few minutes, she took a deep breath, then shared the scene that was unfolding in her mind's eye. With a calm certainty, Carly proceeded to relate a fascinating story which would impact my life in inconceivable ways.

She had found me in a past lifetime in the early 1800s. I was a thirty-three-year-old Chinese man wandering a war-torn countryside on horseback—wounded and starving. My former self, who had stopped to rest on the property of a family of wealth and prestige, was found unconscious by servants who brought him into the home of the affluent family. For three months they nurtured him back to health, after which the head of the household asked for a favor in return: A handwritten message about the wealthy man's impending death to be delivered to his brother, who lived three days away by horseback.

My former self, who was provided with provisions, cash, and a strong horse, sat high and proud in the saddle, grateful for his renewed health and honored to be trusted by the well-respected family. But two days into the journey, while resting for the night, two thieves on horseback threatened to take his horse and belongings at gunpoint. After throwing a distracting punch and kick, he was able to get on his horse and take off, but the angry thieves soon followed on their horses, shooting at him. As the gap between them narrowed, his horse stopped suddenly before a stone wall, catapulting my former self over a cliff and down into a ravine, where he died on impact after breaking every bone in his back.

Carly calmly told me that in order to heal a layer of my current physical pain, my higher self would have to meet my former self at the *death gateway*, a portal to the next life. She believed there is no such thing as the death of a soul, but explained it could be fragmented, and said a part of his soul had been stuck at the death gateway for more than two hundred years because he believed

As Carly talked me through the suspenseful process, while feeling both fear and exhilaration every step of the way, I successfully delivered this message to my former self.

---

his failure to deliver the message had betrayed the family that saved his life.

The task of my higher self was to tell him I am his future self, and that the message was eventually received by his brother—who according to the Akashic records, was able to see the head of the household before he died. My task was to persuade him to go through the death gateway, but not go through it myself, or there could be "devastating consequences."

As Carly talked me through the suspenseful process, while feeling both fear and exhilaration every step of the way, I successfully delivered this message to my former self.

After bringing me back to this earthly plane and re-grounding me through guided imagery, Carly ended our ninety-minute session by asking me to let her know of any noticeable shifts over the next week or two.

I walked around the rest of the day feeling altered, like I was walking on clouds.

The following day I woke up without pain, and over the next three weeks, completely came off all antidepressants, anti-anxiety medication, and muscle relaxants—and have been pain free and unmedicated for thirty years since.

I've questioned if Carly's story was made up or real, but it doesn't matter if she was a true psychic or a creative storyteller, because I am a healthier person thanks to the journey she took me on.

With my mind blown open to the possibilities of healing modalities that I had questioned during my exploration in graduate school, I was now ready to look up a shaman I'd heard so much about. Feeling courageous, and primed for a deeper investigation into my childhood wounding, I wanted to know why there were such huge holes in the memories from my teenage years.

An excellent adventure toward remembering awaited me.

Soul Retrieval

I set out to knock on the doors to my forgotten memories by seeing a different kind of specialist—and in the process, found more motivation to continue exploring and healing from the deepest cuts of my life.

With mile wide gaps in my memory bookending the unforgivable assaults experienced during my young life, I wondered if there was a specific traumatic event which had happened during this time responsible for this mental block. Perhaps these lapses in memory were a form of amnesia from the accumulation of overwhelmingly stressful childhood experiences that I'd dissociated from in order to cope.

I remember events outside of school, but my only memories of my campus experience are of being bullied, of sitting in a classroom on the second floor of a tall building, making a leather visor in an art class, and sitting down to take the graduate equivalency diploma in February of my junior year.

Although I had braved experiential cathartic therapies and traditional conversational counseling for these lapses in memory in my forties, those approaches had been unsuccessful. I had also nervously ventured back to both of my high schools, where I tiptoed around trying to conjure up memories while toting a huge video recorder perched on my shoulder hoping to snag any memory that might lunge at me from buildings I may have spent time in. The campuses were somewhat familiar, but I didn't find any meaningful memories of people, classes, or events.

With no idea what my interests in high school had been, or what kind of student I was, I set out to knock on the doors to my forgotten memories by seeing a different kind of specialist—and in the process, found more motivation to continue exploring and healing from the deepest cuts of my life.

Having briefly learned about shamanic healing in graduate school, I made arrangements to meet with a well-known shaman where I lived, with the intention of being helped to remember.

This shaman believed emotional

or physical trauma in current or previous lifetimes can cause a part of the soul to leave the body to cope with the trauma, and described the soul as our *life force*. She explained how symptoms of soul loss can be disguised as a sense of incompleteness, depression, long term illnesses, and memory loss—but that most of us don't know we have lost a part of our soul and come to accept numbness or lack of meaning in life as normal reality. Her words landed somewhere familiar, as coincidently, while doing some soul searching, I had sensed a hole in my being that happiness seemed to pour through. I just couldn't get full. This searing incompleteness left me empty, even after spending hours with people I love.

The shaman recommended a soul retrieval ceremony, and asked me to bring tobacco as a spirit offering. When she requested that I also bring a personal object, my choice was a favorite heart shaped rock which would be buried in the earth in trade for the return of my missing soul piece.

While I laid on a brightly colored rug from south America, she drummed, rattled, and prayed. I felt completely at ease when she called upon the teacher of my wounding, and I nearly fell asleep as she silently placed her hands on different places of my body for about forty-five minutes.

At the end of the ceremony, kneeling next to me with her face hovering over my heart, she cupped her mouth and breathed the missing part of my soul back into my body with three long expressive exhales which sounded like strong wind. I soon felt a tingling sensation as an overwhelming sense of euphoric contentment and wonder filled my body.

The shaman described traveling through portals of otherworldly realms with her spirit guide Quan Yin, the goddess of compassion, and of finding my missing soul part in the *Cave of the Lost Children*—a place where she said the souls of traumatized children go when seeking safety. She then recounted how the last memory for that child was of her arms wrapped snug around her mother's right leg while waiting on a corner of the busiest intersection in town. Moments later, as a car ripped into both of them, the child was swiftly transported in seemingly liquid form into an eternal darkness where, "Only fear ages. Her soul left the scene on impact." With time stopping for her at age six, it was unclear how long this soul piece had been there, but the shaman said it didn't take much convincing to lure her out.

The shaman then finished up with this message for me from Quan Yin: "Tell her she is free from the prison of the past. Tell her to play with her children, it is in that way she will gain and reintegrate her innocence. It is her time to be born into her power, she is spirit walking the earth in human form. She can call to me at all times, we are as one."

Although the soul retrieval hadn't uncovered any additional buried traumas, I was inspired more than ever to adventure and play with my darling daughters every day. In doing so, my bonds with them deepened, and I was able to play in a way I never had in my own childhood. This shamanic experience also helped me to remember what it was like to be a carefree child playing to my heart's content.

Over the years I have nurtured that cheerful, lighthearted, childlike nature I had forgotten about, which now manifests as playful humor in most aspects of my life, and is a true gift from this shamanic experience.

Nathan Daniel

With everyone swaying into each other, like a kelp garden just under the surface of a churning ocean, many were quietly sobbing, some were shouting, some seemed to have been stunned into silence, and others were openly praying.

The intention I set for my second meeting with the shaman was to find out what was preventing me from loving myself unconditionally. This time, she offered me an overstuffed armchair which felt like it contained a hum from the hundreds of people who'd sat there before me raging, or perhaps spilling grief, as they gripped the arm rests in recognition of their truth. Now that it was my turn, I felt strong and ready.

The shaman sat in front of me and directed me to close my eyes, get comfortable, and take several deep breaths as she prepared me for a journey to the root of my intention. After a ten-minute guided meditation, which created a dreamy state of mind, I became deeply relaxed and soon felt safe and ready to explore.

When she asked me to open the eyes in my mind and describe the scene with all of my senses, I saw myself on a rickety train packed with people of all ages, but with no place to sit. With everyone swaying into each other, like a kelp garden just under the surface of a churning ocean, many were quietly sobbing, some were shouting, some seemed to have been stunned into silence, and others were openly praying. The humid air smelled like sweaty bodies, urine, feces, vomit, and fear, while I did my best to appear calm for my ten-year-old son, who had a firm grip on the satin belt of my wrinkled sunshine yellow dress. Crying from hunger and thirst, when he asked me where we were going, I had no idea, although I knew it couldn't be good since we had been on that train for at least two days.

The shaman then asked me who I was, and where I was traveling from. I didn't know exactly where I had come from, or how long I had been on the train, but knew I was Polish, and worked as a nurse.

Upon arriving at our rural destination with a jolt and much commotion, we were ushered off the train by stern uniformed guards who were carrying rifles.

As we proceeded through a stone archway into a bleak courtyard of a compound resembling a jail, and were put into two lines, an armed guard suddenly grabbed my son and dragged him off. At this point I became hysterical, having lost sight of him but still able to hear him screaming for me. Abruptly pushed into a long line behind an elderly man with a cane, as a young pregnant woman appeared behind me, I began to sob.

Because of my emotional outburst, the shaman reminded me to watch what unfolds as if it was a movie, and encouraged me to feel the arm rests on the chair I was sitting in. She also said I could open my eyes at any time, which I didn't do, but I did try harder to just watch what was going on instead of actually experiencing it.

Soon pushed into a windowless room with cement walls and sprinklers on the ceiling, I felt my face beginning to burn before my lungs did. Covering my face with my hands, I could feel the skin on the tops of my hands burning while people all around me screamed and coughed violently.

I didn't die in that chamber, but was somehow spared, because I found myself in an infirmary, badly burned. When well enough, I was put to work as a nurse, and was able to do simple chores like sharpening needles for injections and cleaning bedpans. Because horrific scars disfigured my face and hands, I was feared and avoided.

An unknown amount of time passed, which felt like years, and I saw myself wearing a black cloak with the hood pulled over most of my face. Crouching down, deeply depressed, leaning on a tall stone wall near a set of steps that led up to a huge building, I could hear children playing.

The shaman then asked me to go up the stairs and describe what I saw and felt.

Gathering my cloak over my right arm, as I slowly made my way up the stairs, I could see it was an orphanage. Standing there in the

> *"Mama, I knew you would come and get me, I've missed you so much!" Not seeing me as the hideous woman I saw myself as, he saw only the love of his life.*

shadows, wanting so desperately to play with the children, I didn't, for fear of my disfigurement scaring them away.

When I saw a preteen boy with a mop of blond hair sitting on a tree stump reading a book, my heart nearly leaped out of my chest—it was my son! He was alive! It was as if the sound of my pounding heart made him look up in my direction, and when he did, I hid my face. But he was curious, and as he started walking toward me, I panicked, wanting to run toward him as much as I wanted to run away. He stood before me silently at first, taking me in as I peeked through the folds of the fabric of my hood. "Mama, is that you?" It took a colossal act of bravery to allow him to see my face, because I expected him to take in a sharp, repulsed breath and run away, but he quickly ran over and wrapped his arms around me. "Mama, I knew you would come and get me, I've missed you so much!" Not seeing me as the hideous woman I saw myself as, he saw only the love of his life.

Choking on my tears, I told the shaman what was unfolding, and she asked me for his name, which I knew instantly: *Nathan Daniel*. When she asked, "Who is he now?" my answer was immediate, and with absolute certainty I said with tearful pride, "My daughter Emily."

But when she then asked, "Who was he before?" and I couldn't find an answer, the shaman did: "This light being came into your life for almost five months in utero."

From this unimaginable experience—made up in my creative mind or not—I shed a layer of defense I had believed was protecting me somehow, and with a growing confidence began to allow people to see me, up close. Meeting people eye-to-eye had never been easy, due to my having suffered from body dysmorphic disorder for many years, but this was the beginning of healing that imagined and preposterous perception of myself.

Wounded Healer

"Compassion was the gift of these lessons, but you had to suffer in order to awaken to your new journey. As a wounded healer, you are now able to go into the deepest pain of others because you have claimed your own."

My second session with the shaman took weeks to emotionally recover from. But, with perfect timing, she invited me to participate in another monumental pilgrimage, this time in a group channeling session—although we hadn't been told who the shaman was going to channel until she opened our circle of six. After sitting in quiet meditation for about fifteen minutes, the shaman took some deep intentional breaths before speaking words of gratitude to Mary Magdalene, whose spirit she had chosen to work with on our behalf.

Surprised to be called on first, I suddenly felt very raw and nervous. Unable to stop adjusting my clothes, and distracted by a few hairs which tickled my forehead, I had no idea where to put my hands. As my eyes squeezed shut in nervous anticipation, fearful thoughts were all that filled my mind: *What if she doesn't respond to the call on my behalf? What if she's busy chatting with another directionless soul in need of answers? Will she really take the time for me?*

After an uncomfortable three minutes of silent wiggling, the shaman started breathing differently, so I opened one eye and saw her hands lift above her head, then over her heart. My spine straightened, and my palms felt sweaty as the shaman began speaking to me.

"Oh, my most beautiful daughter, what a bright one you are. It has taken you great strides to arrive in this place of new destination. Rejoice in the homecoming, for now there is no more to do than to just enjoy the self. You have suffered greatly in order to reach where you now sit, but there is *no thing* to do, as great work has been done already. At this time, your life is a place of rest and safety. You will be solidified as you begin to walk your new path, your brightness shining forth in ways you don't know."

The shaman, whose eyes remained closed, then guided me to ask a question of Mary Magdalene, but not having prepared one, my throat suddenly went dry. Choking on the first question that came to my unsettled mind, I finally spoke.

"Why did I choose this life to reincarnate into?"

My face tightened in anticipation of a painful blow, as if I somehow deserved the misery I'd endured, but an unimaginable narrative ensued instead which detailed the purpose of my suffering. The answer—made up by the shaman or not—was spot on, and shifted me onto a path that would make a positive difference in my life and career in the most profound of ways.

"You needed to know the suffering of a young girl and a woman being abused. You had to feel the fear of rejection, and the fear of telling your truth. You needed to know the suffering of a child of an angry mother, and what it was like to be a lost maiden. Compassion was the gift of these lessons, but you had to suffer in order to awaken to your new journey. As a wounded healer, you are now able to go into the deepest pain of others because you have claimed your own."

Mumbling that I didn't know what it meant to be a wounded healer, after the shaman paused for a moment, clarification soon followed.

"You had to experience, and witness, a multitude of deep suffering so that you may heal others at their deepest levels of pain and suffering."

Her reference to my being a *healer* really didn't make sense to me, because as the health and fitness director at the YMCA, I was always surrounded by people with healthy mindsets. And, being on the verge of a divorce, my thoughts were only of seeking a path to healing myself.

However, fast forward a few years, and the concept of being a healer does indeed fit. After divorcing my husband, graduating from nursing school, and working briefly in cardiology, hospice nursing has provided me with joy (and sustenance) for over fifteen years. Most days of the week you will find me at the bedside of the dying, where I bear witness and facilitate the healing of the deepest forms of pain and suffering—a most sacred work which would be impossible for me to do without having previously endured the painfully difficult experiences I was gifted with before becoming the exuberant person I am today.

"You had to experience, and witness, a multitude of deep suffering so that you may heal others at their deepest levels of pain and suffering."

Walking on Eggshells

I will never again settle in an unhappy relationship for fear of being lonely, or tiptoe around someone else's feelings at my own emotional expense for fear of making them mad or having them abandon me.

They say we choose partners who are similar to one of our parents because we are drawn to the familiar in those relationships, or perhaps for an opportunity to resolve mommy and daddy issues. Only now do I recognize how many similar qualities existed between the man I married, and my detached, uncommunicative, resentfully angry mother.

What did I unlearn from being married to this man? *I will never again settle in an unhappy relationship for fear of being lonely, or tiptoe around someone else's feelings at my own emotional expense for fear of making them mad or having them abandon me.*

When my emotionally distant husband came home in a foul mood, or woke up grumpy, I immediately wondered what I could have done to make him feel that way. When I'd ask him what was wrong, he'd often say, "We'll talk about it later." Sometimes I was left hanging for days, unable to navigate his reactivity if I were to initiate a conversation about what might be going on. His silent treatment had incredible power over me, and his withdrawal felt like a weapon which punished me without confrontation as his non-action battered me into a deeper submission of my wavering self-worth.

I wasn't good at reading his mind, but *was* able to create unnecessary drama in my head when speculating on what was wrong while second guessing myself and dangling in an uncomfortable limbo. The fragility of his mood scared our daughters too, because when he was angry, he would sometimes take a short step toward us with a fist raised over his head. Although he never landed a punch, his emotional blows pummeled my self-confidence. His emotional lashings kept me quietly tiptoeing on eggshells around the house (and his moods) as I did my best to keep the peace. When I'd come home from work, I'd ask the girls how their daddy was doing before I would ask them about their own day. It was all absolutely exhausting. Dependent on him for my emotional wellbeing, it seemed like when he was happy, I was happy.

I became quite good at pretending to be joyous for our daughters (a skill I unknowingly taught them) as I abandoned myself and my own needs for fear of being abandoned by him.

When the stress of this dysfunctional relationship became too much to bear, I made plans to move the girls and I out. Over about six weeks, with the support of my beloved sisterhood of women, I slowly began storing our belongings in a friend's garage so my husband wouldn't notice a big shift all at once. After eventually finding a rental property across town, my girls and I moved out with minimal drama.

Upon leaving, a huge burden was lifted from my shoulders—the rental was *my* home, with *my* rules. My girls felt a sense of freedom in our new place too, we all cried with relief, and I slept for days. It was springtime, and the little garden I soon started in my tiny backyard brought great joy.

After about eight months of separation, my husband started coming around with a new and improved version of himself, which was used to successfully woo us into moving back in with him since I believed it would be best for our daughters for us all to be together.

I couldn't have been more wrong.

His kindness and consideration lasted for only a year. Suddenly becoming spiritually righteous after attending a men's retreat that cracked him open to his pain without providing him with a place to put it, that pain oozed out of him—all over us. Angrier than ever, while constantly reminding us he didn't feel heard, he began to speak in a spiritual psychobabble that was hard to interpret, and which I had no reciprocal language to communicate back with. Speaking his "brutal truth," he became an expert at inflicting pain on others, again without visible bruising. Because I couldn't relate to his new lifestyle and mindset, I withdrew my heart, and our girls did too.

Racking my brain with so many questions, while doubting myself on all levels, I felt stupid and naïve. It also seemed I had lost some hard-earned progress in loving myself. Wondering why I had believed anything would change by going back to him (was I that lonely?), I questioned if I even wanted our relationship to work.

On Christmas morning, as I started down the stairs to open gifts with the girls, he put a hand on my shoulder to stop me, then declared: "When you moved back in, I knew you would leave me again."

When asked why he had lured me back, he told me he was rejecting me so I could see what it felt like to, "stand in the fire of rejection." He added that he wanted to teach me a brutal lesson, then sealed the deal with, "I've lost my desire to adore you."

Spilling my coffee down the front of my white terry cloth robe, I trembled as I squeaked out a forced version of jingle bells to our hysterically happy daughters who were waiting by the Christmas tree. After an excruciating hour of opening gifts, I told him with certainty I was done with our marriage, and wanted a divorce.

During an exceptionally quiet breakfast together the next day, as my husband hovered a syrupy piece of banana pancake in front of his mouth, he said in a matter-of-fact voice, "Tell the girls why you want a divorce."

I could have sworn he had a grin on his face when he made that inappropriately brutal statement before shoving that drippy bite into his mouth and smacking his lips. Feeling sucker punched by his betrayal as our daughters simultaneously shifted their horrified gazes over to me, I'd never felt the heat of such a spotlight before. As I fumbled through my reasons in a language and tone that my young girls could understand, beads of sweat formed on my forehead—while what I really wanted to do was unleash the rage that had been building in my chest, wrap my hands around his version of brutal truth, and strangle it.

Demonstrating to my impressionable young girls how to handle a difficult situation with dignity and grace, I let go of what wasn't serving my heart, or my soul, and walked away from my husband, the dream home we had bought together, and the magnificent garden I had planted and nurtured. After digging up and potting more than twenty favorite plants, I found a ground level apartment to rent, and prioritized giving my girls a magnificent helping of what a peaceful environment looked and felt like.

The fear of the unknown had told me many times it could be worse if I left for good, because there was no guarantee that letting go would land me on solid ground. But now I listened to hope, and my beloved sisterhood, who told me otherwise. Sitting in circles with women, I learned one reason I had chosen to return to this dysfunctional relationship was out of fear that if the relationship didn't work out, maybe none ever would, so I settled to avoid loneliness. It felt strangely safe to stay in the uncomfortable relationship with my husband, perhaps because it was familiar—and perhaps because he paid half the bills.

But returning to my unhappy marriage for the children was a ridiculous attempt at protecting them, and unknowingly taught them how to sacrifice themselves while staying in an unhappy relationship. Children always have at least some sense of what's happening, and they are resilient, but staying longer for their sake could have been worse than the divorce. Regardless of how content I might have pretended to be, our daughters absorbed the impact of the tension that went along with this unhappy marriage well before it ended.

Sitting in circles with women, I learned one reason I had chosen to return to this dysfunctional relationship was out of fear that if the relationship didn't work out, maybe none ever would, so I settled to avoid loneliness.

Leap

Hearing in no uncertain terms that without taking the next steps to heal the wounds of my past I would continue to bleed on my present life, I took a leap into healing the next layer of detrimental patterns I'd developed as a young adult.

A few months after my daughters and I had settled into the new apartment, I sought council for an ever-present hum of angst that continually vibrated in my chest just under my breastbone.

After landing in the care of a person skilled in shadow integration, I was guided through the identification—and, ultimately, exhumation—of dark parts of myself buried in my subconscious that were too uncomfortable to embrace in the light. Hearing in no uncertain terms that without taking the next steps to heal the wounds of my past I would continue to bleed on my present life, I took a leap into healing the next layer of detrimental patterns I'd developed as a young adult.

I did not want to bleed anymore.

But when this facilitator asked me to create a timeline of trauma, from my earliest traumatic memory to the present day, it took a surprising amount of courage to revisit the heartache of my childhood, the humiliation and shame of my teenage years, and the emotional struggles of my adult life.

This painful and exhausting process took over a month to write, and in many cases, felt like a confessional of my sins. I had done quite a bit of work on these experiences already, but as the layers of pain kept peeling away, my deeper discoveries of lies began to reveal many truths as well. Using a yellow legal pad, I was able to chronicle 168 dispiriting circumstances that had shaped my view of myself, and of the world, including: Instances of feeling neglected as a child, being bullied in school, abandonment by my mother, attempting suicide to fit in, manipulating boys to be liked, being raped, my teenage pregnancy, dating with minimal boundaries, the untimely death of my father, how my self-loathing influenced my decision making, staying in dysfunctional relationships, and consequent years of self-abuse with alcohol and drugs.

After reviewing my timeline of trauma, the shadow practitioner had me go back and note which traumas were a result of saying yes, when the better option would have been to say *no*. With a fair number of those instances a result of saying yes to boys and men that used me, she said whenever I'd said yes, when the word no would have better served me, a little bit of my power drained away—which I could completely relate to, because I felt an emptiness that no amount of love or positivity ever seemed to fill.

She explained that the people I had given away my power to still possessed it, and that they had been holding onto it all these years. However, I *could* get it back.

I looked at her dumbfounded, then burst into the same tears that are streaming down my face right now as I write these words. With a fierceness I had never known, I was determined to get my power back, ecstatic at the thought of feeling whole again—and couldn't remember the last time I'd felt intact.

Taking the day off from work at the YMCA to embark on the ceremony she had prescribed to reclaim my power, I cleaned and organized the house, picked flowers from my little potted garden, and made an altar containing symbols of love and strength I had collected. After taking my daughters to school, then sinking into a lavender bath, I sipped chamomile tea to prepare my emotions.

Still, I was nervous. *What if nothing happened? What if my power was being held onto tightly by all those boys and men I'd said yes to? What if I couldn't pry my power out of their grip?* I did my best to let go of those thoughts as I got out of the tub, dried off, and put on a velvety purple gown purchased after giving birth to my second daughter, but which had never been worn.

Laying down on my bed, I adjusted my clothing, and fanned my hair over my pillow. My heart was pounding as I flipped through my timeline of trauma, but could barely see it through the tears welling in my eyes.

The first humiliating entry I was able to focus on was when I was nearing seventeen and at a tailgate party along a two-lane road that paralleled a popular surfing beach. Teenagers, who had parked their borrowed cars up and down both sides of the road with music blaring, were drinking whatever booze they could beg people to buy for them at a nearby 7-11 convenience store.

My girlfriend and I, who were walking up and down the jam-packed road having fun with friends and getting tipsy, were flirting with boys when a well-dressed Hispanic boy emerged from between two cars. After flirting with me for about ten minutes, he asked in broken English if I would go home with him. Although a stranger to me, he looked like a famous boy I'd seen on the cover of Tiger Beat magazine, and had a shy, endearing quality I was instantly attracted to. I don't know what part of me said yes, but I was tipsy on Boones Farm apple wine, and he was cute—but as I climbed into his Ford Pinto, I already felt like I'd made the wrong decision.

Arriving at his house about ten minutes later, I changed my mind, but felt like it was too late to say no because I had already created an expectation, and not wanting to disappoint him, put his needs in front of my own.

Once inside, we walked past his father (who didn't look up at us) who was sitting in the dark living room smoking a cigar watching a Spanish game show on TV. The boy's room was tidy, but smelled like dirty feet, all musty and sour. We stood facing each other for a moment, and I wanted to leave, but didn't know how to act on it as in one quick swoop he pulled my bellbottoms to my knees, flipped me around so my back was to his, and pushed me forward onto his saggy twin bed. Standing behind me, he grabbed my hips, pounded me from behind for about ninety seconds, and was done.

Then, without a word, he brought me back to the beach party, dropping me off where he'd found me. With a sense of embarrassment nobody else could detect, as I stood there, I felt his cum drip down my leg.

Enraged by that memory, a type of volcanic anger I'd never experienced before welled up in me from my lower abdomen. Desperate to finally let go of that yes, and the consequential shame I had carried about it for decades, my whole body became tense as my fists clenched my belly.

Hyperventilating in between sobs, I was startled into the present moment by a tingling sensation and gooey dampness in my crotch, which was followed by an incredible vision: *The increasing wetness was his cum oozing out of me—again!* In my mind's eye it was black and thick like tar, and, moving at the pace of hot lava, was searing a hole through my mattress and dripping onto the floor under my bed.

I envisioned the seemingly endless flow burning through the floor as it sizzled a hole deep into the ground below. Both repulsed and euphoric, I realized what was draining out of me was all the cum and toxic waste from the boys and men I had carelessly said yes to. And I swear I could smell something rotten emanating from my body as this accumulation of shame emptied into the Earth.

At the same time, I could also feel my power trickling back inside me through the crown of my head, and gripping the bed with my fingers and toes, arched my back as I roared like a lion in celebration of this magnificent exchange.

This transcendent release went on for about an hour before I felt both empty and full, after which I slept for the rest of the day.

I could also feel my power trickling back inside me through the crown of my head, and gripping the bed with my fingers and toes, arched my back as I roared like a lion in celebration of this magnificent exchange.

Men Like Him

Then, as a furious heat radiated out in his direction, I opened my mouth and my soul, filled my lungs with air, and screamed, "Fuck you!" as spit flew out of my mouth and onto his face.

Never in my life had I ever screamed, *"Fuck you!"* with the entirety of my body to anyone, let alone out loud in public. All the emotional work I'd been doing, however, had allowed a new layer of volcanic sorrow, stress, overwhelm, and anger laying dormant beneath the surface of my tough exterior to finally have the perfect opportunity to surface.

It was early on a Friday evening, and from my living room window I could see my ex-husband impatiently sitting out front in his old red truck. He had come for our daughters, like he did every other weekend, although they both complained he was too sad, or always lecturing them about his spiritual awakenings, and never wanted to go with him. But in spite of this resistance, on all too many occasions a ridiculous notion of protecting him emotionally had caused me to encourage the girls to go—as if I could have a hand in the three of them developing a loving relationship.

Taking a few deep breaths on my front porch before heading down the driveway, nauseated by nervousness, I was going out to talk with him about my need for more child support. During our divorce settlement, I had reluctantly agreed to a meager $162.50 per child per month because at the time I hadn't had the guts to ask for more. However, this amount had proven to be unfair, since the girls spent most of their time with me.

It hadn't been until after I started nursing school that it became evident his pitifully small amount of monthly support, when added to my my part time salary, wouldn't be enough. Doing my best to make ends meet, I had even taken in an exchange student—with my younger daughter graciously moving into my bedroom closet so we'd have enough space. I had also sold a piece of family heirloom jewelry in order to survive, but that only helped for a few months.

Boldly approaching his truck, my courageous intent quickly morphed into feeling more like a scared puppy with its tail between its legs, and by the time I got to his window, my resolve to be assertive was nearly gone. I *almost* returned to feeling small, meek, and intimidated, but after pulling up some courage from deep down in my nauseated belly, was able to ask him for an extra $100 per month.

With a dominating smirk he huffed, "I'm not giving you any more money, put the girls in the truck, they are spending the weekend with me."

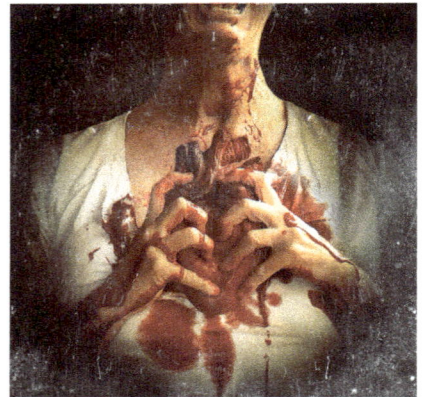

At this point, something inside me shifted, and my blood started to boil. With pins and needles tingling in my fingers and lips, as I looked up from my bare feet and straight into his eyes, I choked out, "No! They don't want to go with you."

His response came through a clenched jaw. "Too bad, they are coming with me. Put them in the truck!"

But after a two-minute speechless standoff, I felt a switch flip on inside of me. With my heart pounding like a drum circle beating wildly in my chest, sweaty palms coiled into fists of rage, as my whole body shook, I stuck my head into the cab of his truck. Then, as a furious heat radiated out in his direction, I opened my mouth and my soul, filled my lungs with air, and screamed, "*Fuck you!*" as spit flew out of my mouth and onto his face. He laughed. I peed my pants.

He later tried to use this "display" of emotion to prove me unsuitable to be raising our daughters; and told people I was a "wounded woman playing victim" in an attempt to make my girls feel sorry for me.

I stormed back into my home, chest heaving in anger, every foot stomp intensifying my resolve to be finished with tiptoeing on eggshells around this bully.

Thank goodness my girls were upstairs, I never wanted to burden them with my adult problems. Running into my downstairs bedroom, after putting a pillow over my face, I screamed and sobbed until my throat felt like it had been scorched by flames.

Quickly finding some composure, I changed my clothes, splashed cool water on my face, and jogged up the stairs to check in with the girls—only to find them gone. I lay down on my older daughter's bed, crying out years of pain and suffering from my marriage, the flood of tears feeling like it spilled off the bed onto to the floor, traveling down the stairs and out into the street until it filled the whole town.

About an hour later, my younger daughter called. "Mama, we're hungry, and there isn't anything to eat in the house."

When I asked where her father was, she said he wasn't home, and a part of me wanted to immediately drive the seven miles to bring them back to our apartment. But not having it in me to confront him again, ordered a pizza to be delivered to them, and asked her older sister to call me if their father didn't come home within the hour, or if either of them didn't feel comfortable being there.

As I hung up the phone, my knees buckled, and falling to the floor I felt a searing pain so deep in my chest I was certain my heart was being ripped out—squeezed bloodless by the hands of my ex-husband who probably felt only joy in causing me to feel like this.

I wanted my babies home with me. They belonged with me, not in an empty home lured by a contentious parent who had forced them to leave my loving arms.

As wounded mama bear noises arose from deep within, my voice bled for my breaking heart, and for all the mothers of children who endure the unbearable heartache of senseless separation and loss.

My ex-husband was busy creating the legacy he is living now.

As wounded mama bear noises arose from deep within, my voice bled for my breaking heart, and for all the mothers of children who endure the unbearable heartache of senseless separation and loss.

The Mystery

There were no expectations of me as I lay there breathing in the mossy smells of the cool moist soil surrounding me, and as I stared up at the sky, watching puffy clouds drift by, I found refuge in the knowledge that nobody knew where I was.

After our dream house sold, with close to $100,000 for a down payment on a home of my own, I was able to purchase a beautiful house thanks to an interest-only loan which did not require documentation of income.

Desperate for a place of my own, I wasn't concerned about the kind of loan it was, but since I was just finishing nursing school, and wasn't sure what my salary would be, the amount was based on guesswork.

Graduating from nursing school around the same time as I received the keys to our new home, I soon found myself struggling to pay the mortgage. Realizing my mistake, when I put the house back on the market after only a year, my realtor said it would most likely sell within three weeks. Little did we know, however, that in three weeks the housing crash of 2008 would occur—and the value of my home would become half of what I had paid for it.

Although not even one offer came in during the ten months it was on the market and I was able to hold it together for another couple of years, when my eldest daughter moved out to go to school in Eugene, I was foreclosed upon after having endured daily threats from the mortgage company. Losing everything, I was left penniless with horrible credit.

I started expressing my struggle with this painful end through the writing of poetry, then through creating conceptual self-portraits to accompany the emotion in the poems. Once I woke to this method of creative self-expression, I was unstoppable, and the pace of my healing accelerated.

It took me three days with a shovel and pickaxe to dig through the cement-like soil in my backyard to make a four-foot deep hole to crawl into for a photo. As I swung that pickaxe over my head and broke through the mortar of the earth with satisfying thuds, it felt like I was digging a grave for the growing sense of inadequacy I was developing as I faced the foreclosure of our home.

My initial intent was to photograph myself in the hole—with the picture accompanying a poem titled "The Mystery" for my self-published book of poetry and photography, *Fear Means Go*—and preparing for this photo turned out to be a cathartic prayer which was answered in a beautiful way.

My camera was secured to a dining room chair perched next to the freshly dug hole, and with my daughters each at a friend's house, I took off all my clothes before gingerly stepping into it. The bottom of the hole was quite cold on my skin as I laid down on my back, so it was hard to relax at first, but I soon felt held and protected by Mother Earth. There were no expectations of me as I lay there breathing in the mossy smells of the cool moist soil surrounding me, and as I stared up at the sky, watching puffy clouds drift by, I found refuge in the knowledge that nobody knew where I was.

Tears of overwhelm silently leaked out of my eyes as I slowly clawed at the earth on either side of me. Hearing waterfalls of little rocks tumbling into the hole every time I reached for the soil around me, I curled up in a ball on my side and prayed for protection and strength to make it through the foreclosure without falling apart. Crying tears of devotion to be the best mother I could be during my transitions, I cried my intent to be able to find peace of heart and mind as the year progressed. Forming little mud puddles where my head lay, I pleaded with Mother Earth to remove my pain, and to recycle my suffering into joy and happiness for myself and my daughters. It felt so good to give my pain to the Earth! Feeling cleansed and drained of tears, I was open and ready to receive any goodness that awaited me.

Then, while considering whether or not it was the right time to sit up and press the timer on the shutter of my camera, I heard the curious voice of my younger daughter.

"Whatcha doin' mom?"

I smiled as I looked up at her eating an orange popsicle.

"Well, I'm laying naked in a hole with my eyes closed."

She clapped her hands and smiled widely, "I want to lay in the hole with you!"

After doing me the favor of pressing the shutter button on the camera, which resulted in just the photograph I needed (and which accompanies this story), within minutes we were both in the hole together, giggling. This beautiful child always has a way of bringing me to joyous present moments in between my struggles.

Feeling renewed, and with a deeper conviction to get myself out of the hole of my making, I opened myself up to the next layer of pain that needed healing—and it was a doozy.

Flaws

This next part of my story is very difficult to talk about, and I've never shared it with anyone, although I probably should have long ago. My belief, however, was that if I said out loud what was really going on inside, I would be judged or laughed at—or, even worse, told I was crazy.

I have come back to life from what seems to have been a long hibernation during which I hid from the light.

After exploring the painful origins of my poor self-worth—and emerging as the authentically beautiful person I always was—I now have an abundance of love and joy to share as a partner, mother, hospice nurse, sister, and friend. The journey to find this true beauty, which took place on one hell of a road, assisted me in a significant amount of unlearning, and I now know that I am not my skin, or the shape of my body.

Trained like so many others to believe I had to look (and be) a certain way in order to be loved, like most women, I also carried shame throughout my life about what I believed was wrong with my body. When women get together, we often share our perceived flaws, and even try to top each other's imperfections. I've asked many women what they would change about their body if they could, with answers ranging from some stating they would *die for* a smaller waistline, the absence of cellulite, bigger boobs, less wrinkles, firmer upper arms, different ears, eyes, chin, feet, longer legs, shorter torso, you name it. Why? *So they would feel more lovable.*

This next part of my story is very difficult to talk about, and I've never shared it with anyone, although I probably should have long ago. My belief, however, was that if I said out loud what was really going on inside, I would be judged or laughed at—or, even worse, told I was crazy.

I suffered from body dysmorphic disorder as a young adult, with its nasty residue affecting my life well into my forties. During the worst of it, I felt ugly, deformed, and monstrous, and hid what I hated the most: my skin, especially on my face. I didn't have acne or scars to hide, just a few freckles and moles, but felt repulsive. Nobody knew this about me as I carried on like a confident person, and I led a double life of self-loathing, all while appearing bold and fearless.

The poor self-concept I experienced as a teen and young adult makes total sense to me now that I have learned that young girls who've been bullied, teased, or abused and who lack the kind of positive reinforcement which develops one's self-worth are at a higher risk for developing body dysmorphic disorder.

As a teenager, I couldn't understand why anyone would want to be my friend because I believed I was physically revolting. I generally avoided mirrors, but when faced with one, would check to see exactly how hideous I was in that moment. With a constant need for reassurance that I actually looked okay, I never really believed any compliments that were offered.

Until I began unlearning my irrational self-judgement, I managed my fear by hiding from the light, afraid to be seen. I didn't avoid social situations, just kept my distance from people because I knew if they got too close, they would examine my atrocious skin and reject me. Back then, it was uncomfortable for me to look anyone in the eye, and I would actually panic—perhaps because my early memories of eye contact weren't loving.

Whenever I was out with a group, I'd be on the lookout for the most flattering light, positioning, and angles to be seen from because I could never relax if the light was too harsh or too revealing. Always making a mad dash to be the first to sit at a restaurant table, I would pick a chair with its back to a window in fear of my perceived flaws being illuminated.

I remember panicking one night when, after having hopped into the front seat of a car with my teenage friends, the dome light came on over my head. All I wanted to do was hide my face in my hands, but instead, immediately looked down and busily dug around in my purse until the car got on the road.

But even when I may not feel attractive externally, I can still emanate beauty.

Overcompensating for my secret by developing perfectionist tendencies, my actions brought attention to my outgoing personality or my athletic abilities, and put my accomplishments in the limelight rather than my perceived flaws.

After my divorce, dating terrified me. I was sure the moles on my skin, my skinny legs, flat butt, and slightly crooked teeth would scare any potential lovers away if they saw me up close; that men would find me unattractive and not worthy of their time. Indeed, I now know that any man who would reject me because of the quality of my skin, the size of my thighs, or the firmness of my butt, is no man I would ever want to be with.

Thankfully, my beloved sisterhood guided me in the first step toward healing this traumatized part of myself. By embracing me and illustrating a path of self-acceptance, this incredible circle of women loved me for *every bit of who I am*, and helped me identify what I found lovable in myself—even when I thought there wasn't much there to love except my accomplishments from overdoing and my dedication to being a caring and devoted mother to my daughters.

After being taught to visualize my love for my daughters as a radiantly beautiful and inextinguishable ember of love in my chest (which I call my *love light*), with practice, I soon grew that ember into a beacon of light that I am able to shine on everyone I meet.

If I find myself feeling unlovable, unworthy, or unattractive, I breathe into this ember of love, feel it expand in my chest, and visualize its beautiful light emanating from my body—and can now do the same with joy.

I can fill a room with love and joy.

Sometimes what I see in the mirror may not reflect how exuberant I feel. The wattle under my chin may squabble to the contrary, and my eyes might argue I look tired even when I am rested; and although I may be confidently holding a strong pose in yoga, the crepe skin on my arms and hands may show I've lived a full life in the sun.

But even when I may not feel attractive externally, I can still emanate beauty. If a mirror tries to tell me malicious things that penetrate my self-acceptance, I tap into my love light and find a confidence inside which shines this beauty from within—and this also helps me care less about what others might think about my appearance.

There will always be those who find something about me that's unattractive, but they are not my people. I appreciate the brand of people who appear in my life and don't cover up their perceived flaws, who exude love and acceptance *no matter what*. These are the ones who give me permission to let the sides of my boobs and freckly crepe skin sag right out from under something sleeveless.

My partner Grant started dating me on the tail end of this path to self-acceptance. By sweet example, he tells me that if I can be kind to and accepting of myself while knowing all my flaws, I can better look at someone else and all their flaws and be accepting of them as well. This is an absolute truth that resonates deeply with me: *Accepting and loving my own flaws has been the gateway to accepting myself and other people.*

Every day, Grant faces me, puts his kind hands on my shoulders, and offers me his loving gaze while saying, "I am here to remind you that you are beautiful," I really do believe him.

But it sure took some doing.

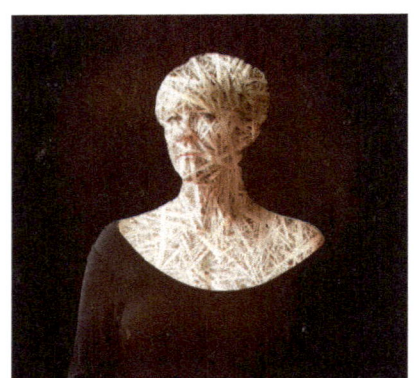

*Accepting and loving my own flaws
has been the gateway to accepting
myself and other people.*

Hard as Nails

Letting go of the need to be good at everything was a tough road, but it led to remarkable self-discovery, and I eventually became more accepting of criticism as I learned it always helps me to learn and grow.

Here is another big truth that is very difficult for me to share, and was hard as nails to unlearn: Most of my adult life, I have been plagued with the paralyzing fear of being perceived as incompetent. My identity and self-worth always depended on my appearing to be good at everything—and occasionally still does. The dread of being perceived as an amateur when I feel like I have redeemable skills at something is exhausting, and I can now see how this sense of inadequacy originated with feeling as if I was *not enough* as a young child.

For decades, my only coping tool for this paralysis was a hammer, so I treated everything like a nail (including myself) by being outwardly defensive, or ridiculously people pleasing, with an internalized sense of ongoing defeat. I've since learned that trying to use one skill, like defensiveness, to deal with all my emotional struggles, was like trying to cook all my food on high—which only works well for some food.

Feeling competent is powerful, and can help me feel impermeable to criticism. When my competence is challenged, however, I can feel threatened *even if I know I'm doing a great job at something,* which often causes me to whip out my hammer in defense. Even playful criticism can be a nail that needs hammering.

My need to be good at everything started waning at age forty-three while in nursing school, where I was mentored in hospitals by older nurses who were known to eat all nursing students alive, regardless of their age. I actually *was* incompetent, and not handling it well emotionally, when a critical teacher urged me to reconsider my choice of pursuing nursing. My first reaction was to defend myself, which quickly morphed into *she thinks I'm not good at this,* so why should I even try? However, later in the day, when I heard that

the teacher had made the same statement to every student (even the hardcore twenty-somethings), I realized she was trying to weed out the insincere among us.

It was my beloved sisterhood who offered me the concept of allowing myself to have a beginner's mind, which I chose to fully embrace, and soon the bold beautiful Mary in me became more determined than ever to succeed. *I knew I had something to offer the world by being a nurse.*

Letting go of the need to be good at everything was a tough road, but it led to remarkable self-discovery, and I eventually became more accepting of criticism as I learned it always helps me to learn and grow.

At this stage of my evolution, I wonder if perhaps I used to see competence as a form of control, understanding as I do now that being less than competent means being vulnerable—which I had believed was a sign of weakness when I was younger. Although I made sure to *pretend* I wasn't afraid to fail, I was always scared as hell under my calm, pseudo-competent exterior.

I have since learned to catch my inner critic in action, and now, when observing myself beginning to beat something up with my hammer, am able to reframe it with a positive perspective. I've given the part of me that carries around my self-doubt and ego the name of Karyl, and often refer to her as my *evil twin*. Karyl also loves to engage in cathartic activities at the gym, like boxing and intense exercise.

More about Karyl and her antics soon.

At this stage of my evolution, I wonder if perhaps I used to see competence as a form of control, understanding as I do now that being less than competent means being vulnerable—which I had believed was a sign of weakness when I was younger.

Wailyn

The sweat of my labor was dripping off my chin onto my heaving chest as I thought triumphantly, maybe now my daughter's cancer will not return!

After stepping into the boxing gym on coveted Wednesday nights, I'd often growl under my breath, *what has to die today?* My favorite punching bag—ragged, and a little soft, so not a favorite of others—always awaited me as it hung from a rusty chain in the corner of a cavernous room smelling of old sweat and ferocity.

I called this bag *Wailyn* because I would wail on that thing with every inch of my might, as if I could actually kill fear or self-doubt with relentless jabs and uppercuts. Wailyn took all my stress, or uncomfortable emotions, and transformed them into glorious release.

One freezing evening in February, I arrived at the gym and decided to kill cancer. After strapping on my azure blue boxing gloves, and easily summoning rage, about forty minutes into my frenzied mission, a series of merciless left hooks busted through one of Wailyn's weak seams. I stopped punching, but the old bag kept swinging as it "bled" all over my feet.

Wailyn had received his last punch. With sandy guts spraying out onto the floor in a spiral pattern like a sand pendulum, I knew he was dying. And that I had killed him. The sweat of my labor was dripping off my chin onto my heaving chest as I thought triumphantly, *maybe now my daughter's cancer will not return!*

Feeling both insanely victorious and pummeled by worry, an urgent need to get outside suddenly came over me. Using my teeth to unfasten the Velcro straps of my gloves, I headed for the exit as if walking away from a plane crash—dazed and numb. Once outside in the icy air, steam instantly rose off my body as my eyes once again spilled tears of grief and worry about the potential of my daughter's health, and I wailed.

On my next Wednesday night visit to the gym, I arranged to spar with the boxing trainer, as I was feeling quite ferocious about slaughtering my self-criticism. The spar, more like an intense choreographed three-minute routine, consisted of a series of eight count combinations of punches thrown in succession, one after the other, with no break in between. The beefy trainer wore foam mitts on his hands to deliver opposing force against my blows, but just one mistake, and I could receive a hit which contained his full strength.

On this night the trainer wore a black hoodie pulled up over his head, which made him look like a faceless monster. Able to insert anybody, any thought, or any thing into the dark space under his hood, I chose the part of me that always criticized how I show up in the world.

He started our intensive match in the middle of the ring, with its fiery pace seeming to bring me to my physical and emotional limits almost immediately. But every time one of my punches landed in the sweet spot on his mitts, and he'd grunt at me like an angry animal ready to tear my head off, it fueled my determination to finish the grueling spar.

After about two minutes, when he backed me into a corner, I suddenly experienced a surprising shift: As I lost track of time, space, and effort, my sense of strength and ability returned, allowing me to reciprocate with vicious animal-like sounds of my own with every punch I threw.

Now on euphoric autopilot, I delivered fierce jabs, hooks, and uppercuts at rapid succession into his mitts, forcing him to take steps backward until we were in the center of the ring again. No thoughts came to mind as everything beyond my body melted away, leaving me ecstatically and deeply connected with the essence of life. With God.

I finished the round feeling incredibly present in my body, and detached from the world around me. Gasping for breath, I numbly thanked the trainer with a wide-eyed bow, quickly turning around as I threw up in my mouth. Ever so slowly making my way to the locker room, I did my best not to appear as dumbfounded as I felt.

After spending a good part of the following week reveling in my experience, I finally concluded: That was the most intense spiritual experience I've ever had.

After spending a good part of the following week reveling in my experience, I finally concluded: *That was the most intense spiritual experience I've ever had.*

Returning to the gym with the intention of having that same mind-blowing spiritual experience again, I was ravenous for another round of blissful awareness which was not of this world but was an ultimate engagement and alignment with spirit.

But the outcome of our next three-minute spar was completely different, and deeply disappointing, as I was trying too hard to duplicate the previous experience. In longing for more, and thinking too much, my ego got in the way, and staying in my head resulted in an excruciating slap to my right ear as I received the full blow of a left hook I was supposed to dodge.

I had learned an important lesson, however, which taught me that sublime experiences can't happen on demand, but must happen organically—like when I'm lost in the rhythmic metronome of moving my body to evocative music; or when glorious hours pass unnoticed while working in the garden or creating art.

No such experience has ever been duplicated sitting still.

Need to be Needed

My daughter was far too alive to die. Beating myself into submission until I didn't have any more tears, I was left with a feeling of empty helplessness that I could barely endure.

This is a story I never before wanted to tell.

I didn't want to collect heartbreaking looks of pity, or gain attention for what had happened, nor did I want to see teary eyed mothers put their hands over their hearts as they knit their eyebrows together in fear that it could happen to their daughters too.

So, in order to avoid awkward silences, and the gasps of mothers who can only muster, "I'm so sorry," through trembling lips, I've kept this torment to myself all these years. But because I am well on the other side of the horror now, it's time to share my journey through an experience which helped me unlearn my self-defeating need to be needed.

My bright and beautiful older daughter, who was finishing up her biochemistry undergraduate degree, had just taken the MCATs in preparation for medical school when she learned something radically different would soon be in store for her.

This discovery, which changed our lives forever (however long *that* might be), occurred during a routine visit to the dermatologist for a rash under her eyes, when the doctor noticed a small but suspicious mole above her left breast. Before we knew it, a moderate portion of that breast had been removed, along with all the lymph nodes under her left arm—because the cancer was there too.

Stage III melanoma typically doesn't have a good outcome. As a hospice nurse, I know this all too well.

The first question my daughter asked the initial oncologist was, "Am I going to lose my hair?" That beautifully thick and shiny mane of blond hair has always been a huge part of her identity; the bumpy purple scars that mark her chest and underarm are now a permanent part of who she is as well.

She soon went in for an MRI, and since I was allowed to be in

the room with her, I stood with my back to the technicians while tenderly holding her feet, all the while trying to tame how violently I was shaking with worry.

Later, she said the bed was vibrating during the scan, which was most likely me, as I trembled while summoning all my angels and spirit guides, all the Gods and all that is good, and imagined her body being filled with white healing light. I'd never been so determined or fierce for anything as I offered her protection the best way I could from whatever that loud, clunky machine would find.

We next made a one-day roundtrip for an appointment in Portland, Oregon that required an exhausting eleven hour drive, but once there, the useless specialist gave us no hope—and charged us $890 for a 24-minute visit. His only suggestions were to get her into some clinical trials, or to have her endure flu-like symptoms for a six-month treatment that might only reduce the recurrence rate of the cancer by about 8%. There was no chemotherapy for this type of cancer, no radiation, and no cure.

I felt powerless when faced with my twenty-three-year-old daughter's cancer diagnosis. All her life, my relentless job had been to fix her problems so she wouldn't have to suffer like I did, and I really didn't know how to not be in control.

I now know that empathy would have been the best option, but back then, she always relied on me for answers and direction. With nothing to *do*, I felt absolutely disabled as a mother, and beat myself up for not having done enough. The anticipatory grief I was feeling numbed my usual compassion, and I felt like a robot with cement blocks strapped to my feet while tending to the dying in my hospice work.

For the next few months, I lived in terror that even with her clear MRI, the cancer could still spread to her organs if just one microscopic cancer cell got past her lymph nodes before they could

It felt like one of those dreams where there was a monster in the basement slowly making its way up the creaky stairs into the house, and although I tried to scream, no sound would come out.

---

be removed. And, to make matters worse, during this period my beloved daughter didn't even want me around! Although my need to be needed was stronger than it had ever been before, she didn't welcome this attention, and felt I was suffocating her by needing to take care of her. Now living with her new boyfriend, she wanted to live a normal life, which left me feeling abandoned as I wallowed in my worry—which I did, like a champion.

Six months after her diagnosis, her local oncologist arranged for her to get a PET scan, during which she was given a dose of a radioactive substance that would render her toxic to me, so I was told to leave for an hour. While in the parking lot, I realized in a panic that if there was a health risk for me to be near her, then she was toxic to herself as well. Sitting in my car, sobbing myself into hysteria while my blood boiled with rage at God, I screamed.

"What have I done? I've allowed these people to poison my baby!"

I started pounding on the steering wheel as I pleaded with my deceased father loud enough so he could hear me in heaven.

"You can't have her yet! She's mine!"

My daughter was far too alive to die. Beating myself into submission until I didn't have any more tears, I was left with a feeling of empty helplessness that I could barely endure.

The next day, the oncologist called my daughter at 7:30 am and left a message to call back to review the results of her PET scan. By noon, my daughter had called back three times, while I had called five times, but neither of us had any luck reaching anyone.

Unable to focus on work that day, I nervously went to the oncology office at lunch time and asked to speak to the doctor or her nurse because my mind was racing down a hundred different rabbit holes, all of which resulted in my daughter's untimely death.

I stood in the waiting room for more than four hours, because I felt that standing was all I could do for my daughter, all the while barely exhaling and unable to contain my fear. When the oncologist stormed into the waiting room waiving papers over her head with an angry look on her face, saying dismissively that my daughter's scans were clear, I was stunned speechless at her awful conduct. Before she grumpily turned around to go back into her office, my wounded mama bear look seemed to cause her to blurt out yet another unkind response.

"I haven't had a moment to come out here to talk to you, I've been so busy, I haven't had lunch or even a moment to pee."

I didn't say a word, and although I wanted to scream at her for the uncaring way she had approached me, instead, I numbly went to the coffee cart in the lobby and bought her a turkey sandwich, which I asked them to make sure she received as soon as possible.

The horror at the possibility of my daughter's cancer returning followed me for the next seven years, and I didn't have the courage to ask the dermatologist about her prognosis at the five-year anniversary because I feared what she might say. Continually bludgeoned by the unknown (*What if one little cancer cell has made its way into her brain and is slowly growing there? She does have migraines ...*) my misery became a permanent bruise deep in the middle of my chest, and an unmovable furrow between my eyebrows. It felt like one of those dreams where there was a monster in the basement slowly making its way up the creaky stairs into the house, and although I tried to scream, no sound would come out.

After those years of exhausting worry wrung out my heart, my beloved sisterhood's advice was to catch myself when creating horror stories about negative outcomes, then to shift my focus by envisioning my daughter happy and healthy well into old age. I eventually got quite good at this, and within a month of this practice, the frequency of these horrible thoughts went from several times per day to only once a day. There were also days when I didn't think of her untimely death at all, and I began to imagine her happily married with twin boys and a daughter of her own.

Seven years, ten months, and thirteen days after her diagnosis, while at a dermatology appointment of my own, I found the courage to ask the same dermatologist who had found the melanoma on my daughter what the chances were of the cancer coming back. The doctor said, "It's my professional opinion, not just my hope, that it's less than one percent." Unable to contain my emotion, I began to cry, and as she stopped what she was doing, I saw her shoulders shake just a little.

I have never exhaled so deeply in my life! That moment marked the end of an era of terror for me.

Within a week of my dermatology appointment, my daughter drove down from central Oregon for a visit. As we sat in the shade of my hazelnut tree sipping peppermint tea, we talked about her cancer experience, and mine. I shared my sense of helplessness, and need to be needed; she spoke of her need for normalcy and independence.

She also explained how she had maintained a positive attitude throughout the whole journey, while I secretly plummeted into pits of despair.

"Mama, you were more helpful than you know. Just knowing you were there, willing to help, I felt supported because I had someone standing by who loved me more than all the stars in the sky, and I knew I could depend on you."

I had been a source of strength for her without doing a thing! And she was able to find comfort in knowing I was her advocate at the ready. I've since been able to share this wonderful sentiment with hundreds of hospice families who feel helpless when faced with what to do for their loved ones who are dying.

My daughter is one of those kind souls who can always find the good in situations, and in people, and who radiates joy and vitality in everything she does. She has an undeniable cheerful greeting if you pass her on the street, which I hope you do some day. Now happily married, she is pregnant with my first grandchild—or maybe twins.

We both believe that a tattoo of a sparrow on her left ribcage, which is accompanied by the words *Love and be Loved* in fancy script under it, is responsible for having saved her life—please ask me about this when I am in your neighborhood giving an author talk about the concepts in this book.

Busy Mind of a Queen Bee

Living in the prison of my head for more than four decades, the queen bee up there could keep my mind and body buzzing for days and nights on end.

If I talked to my friends the way I have talked to myself, I wouldn't have any friends, since I've judged myself more harshly than anyone else ever has. I've spent most of my life with a heavy mind, full of *what if* conspiracies about the health of my body, my family, and the world. Because of that, I have spent a lot of time multi-tasking, over-thinking, and imagining worst-case scenarios about everything I did or should have done.

I've suffered more in my busy mind than I ever have in reality.

The fear of the unknown crippled me into a busyness that I couldn't tame, and in my thirties and forties, it was rare for me to be fully present for long, as I would easily get pulled away from joyous moments by distraction of thought. I wasn't truly listening to anyone, except the voices of doubt in my head.

I began the journey of unlearning this exhausting way of being around the same time that my daughter had been officially cancer-free for one year. Gifting her a trip anywhere in the world to celebrate her life, she chose a yoga retreat at an Ayurvedic spa in Costa Rica. I had about three months to figure out how to do yoga so that I could at least appear competent alongside my daughter. Little did I know, yoga would give me the courage to step out of my head and onto the long hero's journey toward my heart.

Unable to tolerate slow, gentle yoga, my inner athlete needed power flow yoga, which I initially approached from a competitive place. My ego was fed by advanced classes where I could demonstrate my strength and endurance to all the yogis in the room—who weren't even looking at me.

Once, near the end of a difficult sequence of poses in a hot yoga class, we were instructed to quickly lay on our backs in stillness. As I laid there breathing fast, heart pounding and sweat trickling from my temples, the teacher posed a question that shifted my perspective of presence forever.

How do you know you are alive without moving your body or thinking?

My shoulders started shaking as tears filled my ears, and I realized I didn't know how to not move—or stop thinking. Living in the prison of my head for more than four decades, the queen bee up there could keep my mind and body buzzing for days and nights on end.

Relief from my busy mind started taking hold at the end of each yoga session during a few moments of meditative relaxation and integration called *Shavasana*. Typically, I would lay there thinking about something mundane (like what I was going to have for dinner, or whether a bill needed to be paid), but after taking yoga classes for about two months, the teacher's instruction on how to truly relax my mind and let go finally began to make sense. Whenever I caught my mind racing somewhere, I'd acknowledge it, put it aside, and return to a focus on my breath. This worked about twenty percent of the time initially, then grew to most of the time—both on and off the mat—after about six months of practice.

I started participating in international yoga retreats in between local retreats and classes, thinking the pricier retreats could be more meaningful. This journey to presence of mind and heart became expensive, and for

a while, led me down a path of over-spiritualizing my pain. I don't know why I felt I had to leave the country to do yoga, maybe because I thought the farther away I was from where my problems lived, the better it would be, but I couldn't have been more wrong—what ailed me accompanied me everywhere I went.

By bringing my practice home, I realized that traveling the world looking for spiritual connection and peace of mind and heart doesn't compare with the most beautiful of connections that happen when I spend priceless time with the people I love, especially in the simplest of places like my kitchen table and under the hazelnut tree in my back yard.

"How do you know you are alive without moving your body or thinking?"

Carried Away

I had some hard lessons ahead with that unrealistic expectation, like when I tried to "kill" my ego at a spiritual event, failing miserably when my ego didn't die but was bruised and bloodied instead.

In spite of practicing presence of heart and mind, there was a time when I swung to an edge of a disembodied spectrum and found myself using spirituality as both a defense mechanism and a scapegoat. During this same period, I was traveling towards a road of toxic positivity and perpetual optimism thanks to a new teacher who believed I couldn't be well, or happy, unless I rose above negativity.

After dredging the depths of dark memories, and achieving some honesty about what I was feeling, I had reached a limit for the cathartic experiences I tended to gravitate toward, and had begun carrying around spiritual saddle bags into which I stuffed all the emotional issues that would surface during my internal inquiries. However, when those bags became full, I found myself leaking the very pain I was trying to avoid.

Dodging anger, confrontation, or any negative-feeling emotion made me feel safe, at least temporarily, so my goal was to live as though nothing bothered me. I had some hard lessons ahead with that unrealistic expectation, like when I tried to "kill" my ego at a *spiritual* event, failing miserably when my ego didn't die but was bruised and bloodied instead. Thank goodness my spiritual narcissism didn't last long.

By dismissing negative feelings around issues I had no emotional space for with spiritual explanations, I'd gloss over unresolved problems, which then festered without resolution. Breezing past each layer of pain to be unraveled with spiritual copouts, I avoided feelings of anger at all costs. And by simply accepting or rationalizing traumatic experiences for their growth value, I was bypassing them instead of reconciling with what had happened.

It is what it is felt good to say, but didn't help me to discover the root cause of whichever discomfort was presenting itself. I spoke with a conviction of forgiveness, but deep down, I didn't want to forgive. Nor did I really know how.

Although on a spiritual path, I was merely stepping over my pain.

While on this path for a year or so, I used my spiritual practices to increase my self-importance; and by wearing flowing, velvety clothing, tried to send the message that I was quite in tune with my divine femininity. Don't get me wrong, I *am* a divine feminine being, but I don't have to dress a certain way, or speak in enlightened terms, to make sure people perceive me as such.

Spiritual bypassing isn't always a terrible thing. If something bad happens, it may be beneficial to compartmentalize pain that seems too much to deal with in the moment. But, ultimately, my use of bypassing as a long-term solution only proved to create more problems.

I now know that a healthier alternative would have been to *acknowledge my struggles.* In order to heal the pain of my past, I needed to experience and honor my feelings, and be with them wholeheartedly—even if they hurt. More on how I began healing the effects of my trauma with presence coming up soon.

Although on a spiritual path, I was merely stepping over my pain.

Overachiever

It had become exhausting keeping track of all those demanding parts that made up the sum total of me. I lugged around countless versions of myself, and really didn't know who I would be without them.

Intending to impress a coworker with my first book, *Fear Means Go*, a book of poetry and photography, I proudly showed him the cover. Fully expecting to receive a hit of praise, I was taken aback when he said sharply, "Aren't you tired? Don't you ever rest?"

As he dismissed me after that question with a single word, "Overachiever," heat rose up my neck and stung my cheeks as I came back at him defensively.

"No, I'm just a super productive person with many creative outlets."

He didn't buy it, and neither did I.

Having never had the *O* word tossed at me before, I felt deflated, and his comment landed deep in my longing for approval. The awareness of this need for approval took a few more years to root, but with some adventurous nurturing, ultimately revealed some edgy parts of me that needed to stay busy.

For most of my adulthood I wore staying busy as a badge of honor, and wore a shiny crown of the ultimate multitasker with the outward appearance of ease and grace. In reality, I was a great pretender who put on a happy productive face while making myself indispensable in order to receive validation I needed to run the endurance race which was my life.

Until my awareness of this overachieving grew into something I could truly see, I felt important and valuable in staying busy. But by focusing so much on future success, I was neglecting what the present had to offer. Back then, in spite of being desperately lonely, I didn't make the time to be around people—I was just too busy.

It had become exhausting keeping track of all those demanding parts that made up the sum total of me. I lugged around countless versions of myself, and really didn't know who I would be without them.

One night after dinner, my then sixteen-year-old daughter found me sitting at my desk, frustrated about an unkind response to a favorite story I had posted on Facebook. After putting a calm hand on my shoulder she whispered, "Mom, what would happen if you just stopped?"

My response was swift and certain, and without turning around, I mumbled my response.

"I would lose the momentum I have been gathering with all my hard work."

In my head, however, I heard myself give another answer to that overachieving part of me: *I would lose my followers on social media, miss out on speaking gigs, my new hospice portraits book would come to a halt, my garden would die, I would get fat—and I'd become unlovable.*

Later, after sincerely asking myself who I'd be if my busyness as mother, nurse, photographer, writer, social media devotee, public speaker, athlete, yogi, dancer, or gardener ceased, I made an important discovery: *I was a wounded forty-seven-year-old kid, grasping at my need to be accepted and loved.*

After questioning my motives for sharing my photos and stories on social media, I found that I relied on social media "likes" as a meter of my self-worth. I needed external validation to feel deserving, desirable, and valuable, and my worthiness was based on other people's perception of my achievements, not my own.

In my journey to unlearning, it was revealed to me that my overachieving was a form of denial, and it rang true that my addiction to achievement was an attempt at avoiding vulnerability.

At this point I chose to stop taking photographs, writing stories, and sharing anything on social media, which caused me to lose followers and long threads of sweet heartfelt conversations about my hospice portraits and experiences. I also stopped speaking to groups,

I needed external validation to feel deserving, desirable, and valuable, and my worthiness was based on other people's perception of my achievements, not my own.

---

so my books lost sales and momentum—but, as I breathed more deeply, and spent more quality time with my daughters, I began taking peeks into some of the most painful memories of my childhood.

Learning the skills of *not* being busy was quite challenging, although the irritating concept of downtime allowing me to reflect on my life continued to be offered by my sisterhood. Facing my life's history frightened me, because it meant I would have to face the truths of my upbringing while feeling all the unresolved pain I had stuffed into convenient little compartments somewhere deep in my people pleasing vault.

With the ongoing support of my beloved sisterhood assisting me in finding enough courage to do the hard work of revisiting my childhood trauma, I was able to unlearn more of the values I had adopted as a child which had shaped my view of the world and influenced my future decision making.

This was the point at which I started looking within for my self-worth.

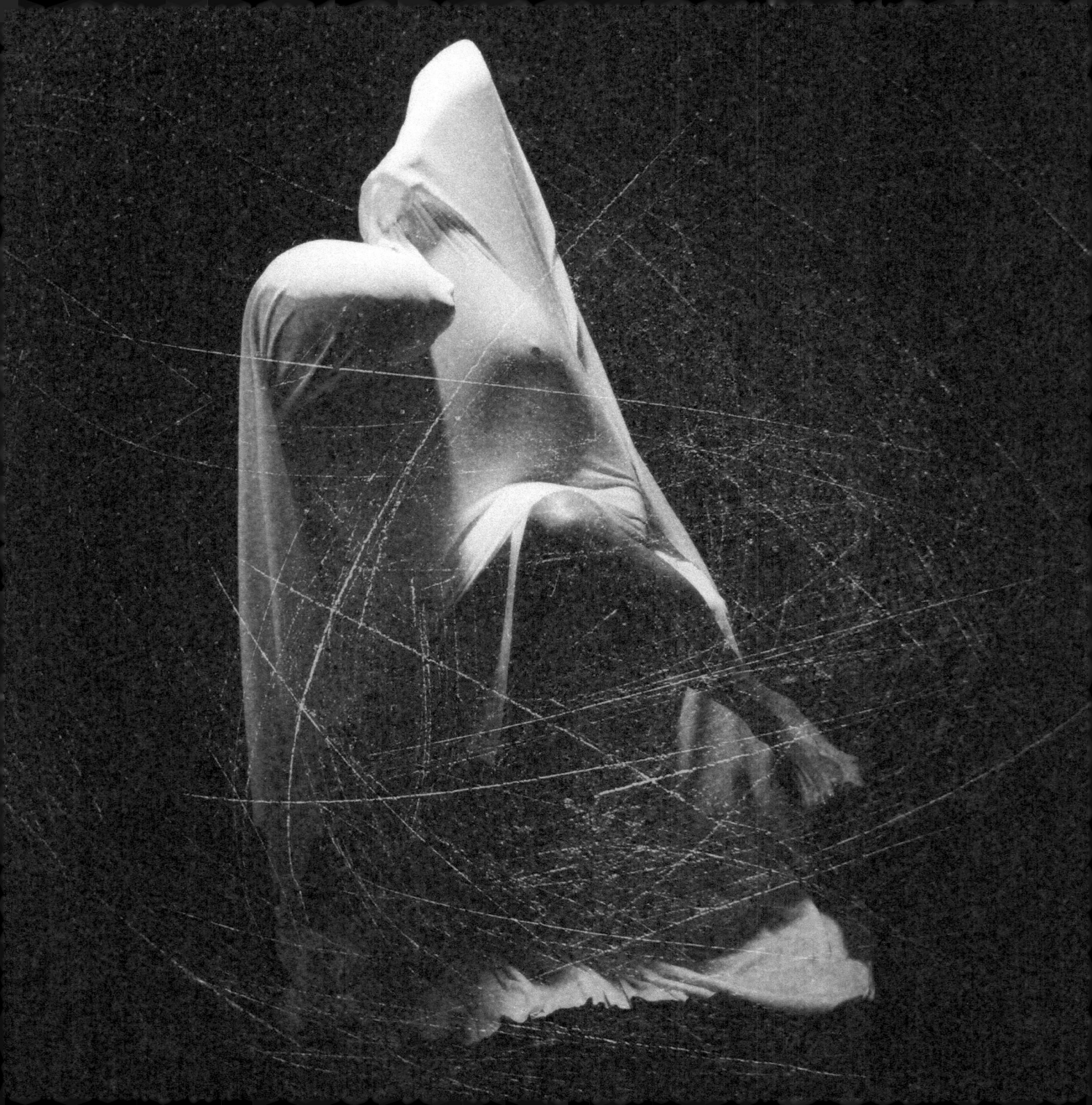

Imposter Syndrome

Believing that my successes were akin to good timing or strokes of luck, I often felt like an imposter, fearful that at any moment someone would roll me over, take a closer look, and find out I was a fraud.

One morning over breakfast, a dear friend casually said, "You could have easily turned out to be one of those arrogant and egotistical snobs with all that you've accomplished." But I honestly didn't know what he was talking about.

I have experienced a lot of success in my adult life, and for the most part, overtly. That said, it's been a long pilgrimage of being loved unconditionally by a handful of amazing women, and one man, for me to finally internalize my accomplishments.

For years, I seriously wondered what gave me the right to call myself an artist, writer, photographer, athlete, and musician, or a smart, capable, and confident woman.

Certain that my achievements had nothing to do with my talents, strengths, or abilities, I felt like I was fooling the people who loved and admired me. Believing that my successes were akin to good timing or strokes of luck, I often felt like an imposter, fearful that at any moment someone would roll me over, take a closer look, and find out I was a fraud.

The Imposter Syndrome is real, especially for successful women, but what is it that makes high achieving women suffer from this type of inadequacy and chronic self-doubt? Why do we question our intelligence and abilities? Is this way of thinking linked to perfectionism? Can I reach out and wag my finger of blame at someone for this self-deprecating syndrome that bulldozed me into thinking I wasn't good enough?

Despite having had very successful art shows, deep inside I felt like a lucky fraud posing as an artist. And even though I've had a couple of books published, the belief that I was an unskilled writer who could take an entire day to write just one paragraph was very real.

People have called me a chef because I was *The Everyday Gourmet* on a local ABC television affiliate, with cooking segments

taped in my gourmet kitchen which replaced *The Galloping Gourmet* for two holiday seasons. To me, however, it felt like a lucky break—anyone can follow a recipe, right?

I've assumed that the success I experienced in school was due to my being able to complete the coursework and submit all the pieces of paper that documented the hours I had put in. I've received a master's degree in public health and two bachelor's degrees—one in exercise science, and the other in nursing. But just because I've been able to pull those off, does that make me smart and confident?

I was Hawaii state arm wrestling champion, competed in marathons and triathlons, and hold a world championship gold medal in juggling. Does this make me an athlete, or did I just show up in decent enough shape to compete?

Even with all of my successes, I only felt fleeting happiness, believing that to be loved I had to regularly achieve something on a grand scale. I actually felt stress when I wasn't accomplishing anything.

In exploring the roots of this belief system, I was asked to consider what unmet needs could have prompted this way of thinking, and the answer was hair raising: My self-image had been built and maintained from a place of lack due to not having received the love I needed as a child.

Thankfully, I eventually learned how to fill in the blank of this statement: *If I'm n<u>ot achieving</u> something, I'm not enough.* With a goal of figuring out how to feel like I was enough without any external achievement, the answer to that question turned out to be excruciatingly challenging, as I needed validation that I was good enough, which would in turn make me lovable enough.

My first step in stopping myself from feeling like a fraud was to stop thinking like one. I learned that the brain will adopt new ways of thinking if a new thought pattern is repeated enough times (positive or negative). It may be a *fake it until you make it* mentality, but it works. So, daily, I affirmed out loud that I was a smart, capable woman with many talents, open to receiving an abundance of love regardless of my achievements. It was a rough start, but after a couple of months I began to believe that maybe I didn't have to earn respect or rely on what other people thought about me in order to feel valued.

I realize now that I don't have to do anything spectacular to be loved, I just have to be me. And while my achievements are not the path to being lovable, being my spectacular authentic self is the greatest service I can offer to the world.

PART THREE
Transcendence

Take Up Space

An adventurous woman I work with in hospice invited me to join her and two other like-minded colleagues at a private Wild Women Dance. The ceremony was to be facilitated by a shamanic movement therapist who was going to host the dance in a small studio in her home, and although I didn't expect anything monumental to happen, at the very least, it sounded like a fun bonding experience for the four of us.

However, much to my surprise, a colossal shift in perspective was in store for me that evening—one that would heal a part of me with the grand inspiration to do everything differently, and with as much passion as I could evoke.

While driving to the dance, I struggled with arriving at an intention, and in going through those bones of contention I'd like to be better, different, or gone, had quite a conversation with myself as I maneuvered through traffic. While pondering the question of what was in the way of my being happier, more content, wiser, healthier, calmer, more creative and less critical, I was unable to settle on any one thing, but as I pulled up to my destination, my intention suddenly became crystal clear: *What is in my way?*

So, for this dance, I invited whatever was in my way to be revealed to me.

In the sweet and vulnerable opening circle, we shared what was going on in our lives, each saying our intentions out loud like a prayer as we called in our spirit guides to join us in the dance. After being instructed to put on blindfolds before the music started so we'd be in our bodies instead of outwardly connecting with each other, the facilitator gave us permission to fully express whatever emotion the music elicited in us. She also encouraged us to move around the room with complete freedom, promising to prevent us from bumping into each other since she was not wearing a blindfold.

Her captivating playlist instantly invited reflection as she guided us to go within. As the outer world quickly dropped away, her hypnotic musical choices carried me into a trance-like state. One minute I was ecstatically swirling around like a whirling dervish; then I was inspired to jump up and down in place, spellbound by African rhythms.

About thirty minutes in, Native American drums took me over an emotional and physical edge. My body started shaking violently, and it felt like my head was spinning around on my neck, but I felt courageous enough to ask the spirit guides I had called in to answer my question: *What is in my way?*

By now, my blindfold had become saturated with sweat, and my hair was sticking to my face and neck. When I heard nothing in response, even after asking several more times, I became more and more impatient with each unanswered request. Thinking perhaps I needed to move my body faster and harder in order to earn the answer, I was soon out of breath, and so dizzy it felt like I might vomit. The answer to my question only came to me when I was forced by my body to stop moving.

I am in my way.

I think my heart already knew that, since the answers we seek usually reside there—if we can only stop, and truly listen.

As I stood there dripping sweat onto the floor, another message emerged, loud and clear.

Take up space, be big, be seen, be heard!

My next breathless question was *how*? Having typically walked through life trying to create as little disturbance as possible, being big and taking up space without being obnoxious was not my norm.

Then, upon hearing *take up space with your presence and words, your voice is valid,* the fearless thoughts that came through caused me to howl with my entire being. Crying with laughter, and whooping out loud in recognition of my new truth, as the other women in the studio instantly joined in, we sounded like a pack of wild animal women celebrating life.

The transformative ceremony had transcended dance. And with the guidance, music, and movement medicinal on so many levels, I emerged with an exhilarating confidence.

This experience inspired me to unlearn my habit of withholding ideas; and soon after, I began working in earnest on this book. In the past I had believed that I could avoid getting hurt by not using my voice, but now, having been encouraged to stop apologizing for the way I express myself, I was also able to stop tip-toeing around conflict.

No more feeling small for this girl! I am now happily taking up space with my body, my words, and my art.

About thirty minutes in, Native American drums took me over an emotional and physical edge. My body started shaking violently, and it felt like my head was spinning around on my neck, but I felt courageous enough to ask the spirit guides I had called in to answer my question: What is in my way?

To Be Vulnerable

Before my painfully intimidating and heart-opening exploration of vulnerability—and before my current loving relationship—my fear of rejection was so great, I believed showing up perfect in all ways would minimize judgement, as well as the potential for exclusion.

I've discovered that in order to allow anyone to really get to know me, I must be vulnerable enough to share the parts of me that I love, as well as any parts I don't love—and, thanks to finding my way to being vulnerable, I've been able to attract the greatest love of my life, *me*.

My incredible partner, who ties for first place as the greatest love of my life, tells me it's my imperfections that make me perfectly me, and that by accepting them in myself, I will be better able to accept the imperfections of others. This is a truth I am constantly learning.

Recently, when I complained about my aging body, he stroked my cheek and gazed affectionately into my eyes, responding, "I love you *because* you are sixty." This lovingly demonstrated not only something that causes me to feel vulnerable, but also that which makes me beautiful and most lovable to him.

Before my painfully intimidating and heart-opening exploration of vulnerability—and before my current loving relationship—my fear of rejection was so great, I believed showing up perfect in all ways would minimize judgement, as well as the potential for exclusion.

For instance, just in case someone might drop by, or when leaving my home for any reason—even just to go to the grocery store—I always wore clothes that drew compliments, along with foundation, lipstick, and mascara, and I made sure my hair was sprayed perfectly in place. I also carried a powder compact with a mirror, and checked regularly for shiny spots on my nose and chin. I even took this compact with me on hikes with friends and to family gatherings, because I felt too vulnerable without it.

A big vulnerability breakthrough occurred when I took both of my daughters to a yoga retreat in Central America to celebrate their brave and courageous lives, and to honor our love for each other. I debated bringing any makeup, and while holding a bottle of Revlon in my hand, staring at it with my heart aflutter, wondered if I'd be okay without it. *Could I actually allow myself to be completely seen?* I knew what I would look like without my small arsenal of beauty products: My droopy right eyelid would be swallowed by my ruddy complexion, and my pale thin lips would disappear completely, rendering me into one of those awful before pictures of a woman getting ready for a makeover. I felt the potential of being judged as "worn out," and feared being dismissed by the younger participants at the retreat.

Although I did bring the makeup, after deciding not to use it I experienced an immediate withdrawal, and had a few panicky moments when I believed the little spider veins on my face were glowing in all their purple and red glory. With no place to hide, I felt claustrophobic in my own skin as I sat in small groups with other yogis who spoke about the evolution of their lives through yoga.

However, the most revealing moment of the entire retreat took place just as I was about to receive a massage, when the therapist took my left arm in her hands and said sweetly, "You have skin just like mine." After raising my head just a little, and quickly glancing at the crepe paper, sun-damaged skin hanging from her forearms, I fell back onto the massage table with a sudden realization: *Oh, dear Lord, I do!*

That innocent comment turned out to be an initiation into a deeper sense of authenticity. Sure, I looked like all the other plain, fifty-something-year-old women at the retreat with thinning skin and age spots on display, but I was also tired of trying to hide my skin, so I chose to amble around the retreat grounds in practically nothing—and makeup free.

As it turned out, nobody ran away or hid when they caught a glimpse of me, and my daughters didn't treat me any differently without the usual makeup, fully exposed. In fact, while blending in seamlessly with the all-natural crowd, from that moment forward I began to feel totally accepted for the "version" of myself I almost hadn't brought with me! The release of the burden to appear perfect was almost orgasmic.

Upon returning to the US, after looking deeply into how numbing the pursuit of perfection can be, I soon understood that it is an exhausting approach to life which can also numb the vast potentials that await me—including the expression of pure joy.

I now understand that being vulnerable is *not* a sign of weakness. In reality, it is a sign of strength to be willing to follow my heart's desires without requiring any guarantees. The nervous feeling that arises before taking any perceived risk is really vulnerability encouraging me to take the next step forward. Loving fully, with my heart nervously aflutter in my chest, is vulnerability inviting me to open my heart even wider.

Being vulnerable is a risk to those carefully protected parts of myself left tender by past experiences that had made me want to hide my true self. While sharing how I really feel with someone could certainly result in what feels like a stab to my heart, it is really my ego which would receive the impact.

Putting my creative self out there with the possibility of judgement was scary because I felt like a failure if others didn't appreciate my artform, but that no longer matters. I now make my art for myself, and for whomever else might be in need of its message.

For me, vulnerability has evolved into exposing the underbelly of my truest and most authentic self regardless of the potential of it being ripped into by people who don't understand me.

With this book, I stand before the world with my lifetime of experiences and pain in full view for all to see. Showing up in my entirety—naked, raw, and transparent—I am curious as to who will be left standing before me.

Previously, the fear of rejection and judgment prevented me from taking any risk; pretending to be someone else as I sought acceptance and love seemed so much easier. Now, showing up with my vulnerability intact is worth whatever risk that might entail, and I look forward to seeing who will stick around to love and support me for who *I really am*. Every bit of me.

Trust the Struggle

"I am not in alignment with my highest purpose, so I QUIT!" With my arms flying over my head in resolution, and tears flowing down my cheeks, the crowd of people erupted in wild applause as they gave me a standing ovation.

Before arriving at a new and improved version of my authentic self, unlearning a *grass is always greener* mindset was required. Indeed, it was only after uprooting my life, and moving hundreds of miles away, that I was able to remember how valuable and full of purpose my life here in Southern Oregon really is.

My journey to remembering started on a sweltering day in August of 2016, when I had put an oven thermometer in my car to see just how damn hot it was in there. A typical workday would include my getting in and out of the car at least five times when seeing patients, and on this particular day, as the fire season raged and the skies were filled with dense smoke and ash, the average temperature inside my parked car was a sizzling 161 degrees. On days like these, I would heat up my lunch on the dashboard while inside a patient's home.

So, as I sat in my oven of a car recalling a glorious tour of the Olympic Peninsula the previous summer, I decided to look up that area's weather on my phone. Having been quite charmed at that time by the Puget Sound—with its temperate climate, ferry rides, and pristine nature—I let out a shrill sound that probably only dogs could hear after reading they were currently experiencing a balmy 68 degrees with light cloud cover.

Easily finding a Seattle hospice online, I immediately called to inquire about the possibility of any openings they might have for registered nurses. To my delight, they had a clinical practice management position available, and I was up there within two weeks for an interview. Right up front, they mentioned that *some* of their staff had been developing bitter temperaments, so after earnestly pitching my idea of bringing the heart of healthcare back to their organization, they hired me on the spot. They needed me, and the remnants of the egoic overachiever part of me needed them.

During my move to Seattle the following October, I had the foolish notion of being a knight in shining armor who would make a monumental difference in the morale of their staff just by being myself.

I couldn't have been more wrong, and later learned that my desire to save these people was more ego driven than heartfelt aspiration.

Although my new job sounded like a dream come true—with all the promised opportunities to educate and nurture the other nurses on staff—it turned out to be a nightmare. The business was operating out of compliance, and nobody liked or supported each other in that awful fluorescent lit office located next to a paper mill that made the stuffy office smell like rotten broccoli.

During my first month, I had happily taken every nurse out to lunch individually (at my own expense). After asking each of them what was, and wasn't, working in their hospice, the consensus was clear: *Nothing there worked, and all thirteen of them didn't care.*

To make matters worse, upper management didn't provide me with any opportunities to do meaningful interventions with the nurses, or to interact with patients and families. Instead, I was given meaningless administrative tasks that anybody could do, all while overhearing cringeworthy backstabbing office gossip. Not only were they not following through with the seductive job description they promised me, they weren't using me for my talents and skills. Within three months I realized there would be no way to make a difference there.

Angry and resentful, I cried on the way to and from work every day, didn't eat much, was exhausted all the time, and began to appear gaunt. Much later, I realized my body was saying *NO* to my decision to move to Seattle well before my mind had allowed my heart to agree—and the body never lies.

On one occasion, after complaining about these circumstances to one of my beloved friends in Oregon on the phone, she asked if life had ever handed me what I really wanted, then added that by resisting the struggle, I might never learn the lessons being offered in Washington.

Grumbling that I didn't deserve my current situation, she countered with, "It's not about deserving, it's about humanity; and since you are a human, there is no way around it." She then offered me a perfect opportunity to be present and patient with my suffering by giving me a new mantra: *Trust the struggle.*

So, I wrote the acronym TTS on a yellow sticky note and put it at eye level on my work computer. Then, when I began believing the horrible office environment I was working in could be worth the positive resolution I was seeking, something extraordinary happened.

In February of 2017, the American Academy of Hospice and Palliative Care Medicine flew me to their annual conference in Phoenix, Arizona in honor of my hospice photography which had been chosen for all twelve covers of their international journals for 2016. The best moment of the conference, however, did not occur during recognition of my photography work or my hospice portraits book, but with a simple yet powerful statement a speaker shared at the end of her seminar on productivity.

"The only way to do great work is to love what you do."

My heart vaulted up into my throat, and although I wanted to shout in recognition of this truth, all I could do was grip my chair with both hands and breathlessly stare dumbfounded at the floor in front of my feet as people lined up at microphones to ask questions.

After about ten minutes I was roused out of my immobile stupor when the speaker announced time for just one more question or comment. Looking to my right, I saw an empty microphone in the front of the room, and with my heart beating wildly, leapt to my feet and began to approach it—although I didn't know what I was going to say. It took every ounce of emotional strength I had to not burst into tears when I became fully aware of what I needed to articulate, and after two deep breaths and a glance over the heads of the 400 people staring at me, I was finally able to speak.

"Last October I uprooted from an incredible community, a meaningful job, family and dear friends, to pursue a management position in a hospice in Washington that I thought was the next logical step in my career. This job looks great on paper, brings me a six-figure income, but I am not happy! I am unable to do great work, because I am not loving what I am doing there.

I am not in alignment with my highest purpose, so I QUIT!" With my arms flying over my head in resolution, and tears flowing down my cheeks, the crowd of people erupted in wild applause as they gave me a standing ovation. After the applause calmed, and I had stopped crying enough to continue speaking, I completed my thought.

"What I love is being a home hospice nurse. I want to go back to sitting at the bedside of the dying to help them release the past, detach from the future, and find peace of heart and mind. I am good at helping people get to what matters most, and to me that is love and connection."

I went on to describe more about why I love hospice nursing, taking photographs of the dying holding hands with their beloveds, and my plans for speaking publicly about what I know to be true. It felt so good to say those things out loud to this group, and to the Universe. I felt seen and heard, and received a big YES in my body, heart, and soul in regard to making the choice to leave Seattle.

Soon swarmed by hospice workers who offered me congratulations as well as job offers all over the country, what I *really* wanted was to ask my former supervisor from the hospice in Oregon (who was at the conference) if she would take me back. After quickly finding her, she took me in her arms with a simple, "Welcome home," and I was back in Oregon working as a hospice RN by early May.

It had taken leaving Oregon, the work I love, and my dear community to find the clarity needed regarding the highest and best use of my gifts—I had to walk away from my calling in order to be called into remembrance of my true purpose in life.

*"The only way to do great work
is to love what you do."*

Subrosa

This was the beginning of learning that there is a way to hold grief and gratitude at the same time. It's easy to be grateful when I am belly up to a Thanksgiving table, but finding gratitude when a situation renders strong negative emotions can be a monumental task.

Pain is certainly an inevitable part of life. However, I now understand that in the past I chose to *suffer*, because I didn't know suffering was optional. On some days, I rolled out of bed in survival mode expecting the worst to happen, because it usually did. In the hardest of times, I faced my day with dread, which I was good at because I had grown a skill set for how to suffer in big ways. Suffering was so familiar, if there was nothing wrong in the moment, I would look for something to confirm that my life sucked.

I have since learned I can also anticipate positive experiences, and am now able to look for the good in the world as well.

In exploring my old Eeyore mindset, I've come to see how allowing myself to feel defeated before the start of my day was dooming. It seemed absurd that doing the opposite, which was conjuring up a sense of hope to propel me into my day, would change anything. I scoffed at the idea of making an intentional choice to be hopeful, even if I knew my day was going to be difficult. The part of me identifying with suffering just could not relate, plus it seemed too difficult, and unnatural, to embrace this concept.

For instance, on a particularly dreary morning before going to the office I dreaded in Seattle, I lay in bed reluctant to face the predictably awful day ahead of me. For years I had been told *I am not my thoughts*, but that part of me that was comfortable wallowing wasn't having any of it. Because I was miserable and unhappy, miserable and unhappy thoughts and actions felt fitting to wear that day.

Even though my alarm had already rung twice, I begrudgingly decided not to get out of bed until I was able to find a nugget of something to be upbeat about. Searching every inch of the ceiling above my bed for something positive that might fuel a hopeful intention for the day, I noticed an ancient spider web up in the corner of my room which ultimately held the answer: Like the spiders up there out of my reach, I felt physically safe, so I got out of bed and spent the day repeating *I am safe* until my eye-rolling about the intention stopped, and I soon started feeling gratitude for my safety. Gratitude then became my daily mantra, which it still is to this day.

This was the beginning of learning that there is a way to hold grief *and* gratitude at the same time. It's easy to be grateful when I am belly up to a Thanksgiving table, but finding gratitude when a situation renders strong negative emotions can be a monumental task.

In fact, as I write this, most of the northwestern US is on fire, the air quality where I live in Oregon is unbreathable, it's been over 100 degrees outside for weeks, and COVID is making a vengeful fourth comeback which is devastating the healthcare system where I work. When visiting families in their stifling, unairconditioned smokey homes, my lungs burn and my eyes sting while I'm surrounded by overwhelmed angry people who have nowhere to put their feelings but in my lap when I take a seat next to a deathbed.

I am also loved and cared about by my magnificent family and beloved friends who would drop anything to come to my aid. I celebrate eating from my garden every day, and get to spend quality alone time in my airconditioned studio creating art while breathing filtered air. My healthy lifestyle allows me to sleep well, my strong body welcomes daily morning workouts with my beloved daughter, I'm going to be a grandmother soon, and with my adventurous spirit I can get in my car and drive anywhere I want.

I have discovered the circumstances I am sad or angry about can live right alongside what brings me happiness and hope, but it is up to me to choose where I want to dwell. And although I might not always see the brighter side, I now have the tools to do so.

*I have discovered the circumstances
I am sad or angry about can live right
alongside what brings me happiness
and hope, but it is up to me to choose
where I want to dwell.*

Calling in Joy

Where does my joy go when I struggle? It is always there, just waiting to be remembered—so I do my best to remember that I choose my joyous attitude, it doesn't choose me.

I'm continually inspired by those bright light people who beam joy, love, and gratitude despite incredible disparity. I often find these phenomenal people, who I refer to as *joy radiators,* in hospice care at the end of their lives. Although all too often living in substandard environments without many physical possessions, these unique individuals still find a way to wholeheartedly give of themselves in spite of the ugly face of ravaging disease or pain. Perhaps it's due to their previous exposure to hardships that they have greater empathy, or maybe it's their true nature to be inspiringly happy. Nevertheless, I stumble out of their homes inoculated with an uplifted spirit, motivated to be more like them while I am still very much alive and thriving in my fortunate world. It is because of these joy radiators that I have vowed to live my life in service of love and joy as much as possible.

Where does my joy go when I struggle? It is always there, just waiting to be remembered—so I do my best to remember that I choose my joyous attitude, it doesn't choose me. Opting for an upbeat mindset can set the stage for my day, and choosing joy is a good resource to cultivate and draw from when life delivers unhappy circumstances. Even if my day turns a corner, and becomes a shitshow, a joyous attitude can help me navigate the crap.

I have been judged for being too joyous, and have even been called *fake happy,* probably because being happy most of the time can be perceived as trivializing life since there is so much to be concerned and upset about.

The reality is though, by outwardly practicing loving optimism and joy, I can sometimes inspire others to feel more more joyous as well. With most people responding well to love and acts of kindness, especially when they recognize it in themselves, joy can actually be a contagious superpower. If I project anger, that's what I will most likely get in return, and I often receive confirmation of my current state of mind when I share it with others. I now understand that a joyous attitude is a choice we all can make—as is optimism, kindness, and respect.

Once I discovered that by being grateful, I am calling in joy, I began the practice of starting each day by writing down at least five things I am grateful for. This practice sets a tone of gratitude and joy for my whole day.

Finding ways to express gratitude toward people without using the words *thank you* by saying exactly what I appreciate about them will lift their spirits, and consequently, my joy gets bolstered as well.

Because joy is cultivated by making time to be in places that align with my passions, I am in joy heaven when deep in the creative process of writing or making conceptual portraits, when hours have flown by while gardening,

in spending time loving and laughing with the people I care about, and when I am speaking to groups of people about what I know to be true.

At the bedside of the dying, while offering counsel to families, I pause in silent recognition of the difference I am making in their lives. This acknowledgment of the positive impact I am having in the lives of my patients and families further nourishes my joy.

In doing what I love, I am cultivating joy.

With most people responding well to love and acts of kindness, especially when they recognize it in themselves, joy can actually be a contagious superpower.

Running Out of Steam

This is a place where many of us end up when we have been doing so much for others that we find ourselves with nothing left to give, although we do our best to rise up somehow and continue. The outcome is predictable, yet somehow surprising.

My work in hospice, although extremely gratifying, started to take a toll on me during a time when I was juggling up to fourteen critical needs patients and families—all of whom needed me to provide comprehensive remedies for complex pain first thing, every morning. The accumulation of stress I experienced tending to people who suffered unimaginable agony left me emotionally and physically frazzled.

At the same time, my family also needed my undivided attention in ways I could barely keep up with. One of my daughters had been in and out of the ER with unexplainable abdominal pain, while my other daughter was having an existential crisis which was the result of a significant emotional event. I always showed up for my daughters, but would be in an exhausted state when doing so.

I was trying to ease the pain in too many people, at my personal expense, and because I was neglecting my own pain, was running on empty. Although I'd hope for a good night's sleep, which in all likelihood would only put fumes into my tank, I rarely slept at all. My partner soon came to recognize the irritable *weepy zombie* in me when I'd walk in the door at the end of a long workday.

One super busy day, I ran out of gas before work, and the friend I had called to rescue me greeted with an emphatic, "Can't drive a car without fuel, Mary. Too busy driving to stop for gas, huh?" Then, when she offered the observation that I was burning out, I argued to the contrary like a sleepy toddler who didn't want to take a nap.

My constant fatigue prevented me from engaging in any of my passions, and my joyous attitude waivered, but I didn't have the energy to spend time with the people that usually lift me up. Not making the best decisions for my own emotional and physical health, I was running full steam toward a head-on collision, until I finally realized my only choice was to *stop*.

Having reached my tipping point, I scrambled to a beloved neighbor's house, fell to my knees, and let out some primal screams that pierced the floor to the Earth's core. I felt better, and was acutely aware of how tired I was on all levels.

The need to practice better self-care was becoming more obvious, but I felt like taking care of myself first would mean I was putting the care of the people I loved the most last. I was placing my daughters wellbeing ahead of my own, my patients got what was left, while my loving partner was prioritizing me, like good partners do.

As it turned out, my burnout was a result of *compassion fatigue*, which happens to caregivers as a result of prolonged exposure to suffering. The cumulative effect of managing, or being witness to, trauma can lead to emotional and physical exhaustion—which can happen suddenly, because there is a limit to what we can handle.

This is a place where many of us end up when we have been doing so much for others that we find ourselves with nothing left to give, although we do our best to rise up somehow and continue. The outcome is predictable, yet somehow surprising: We get so wrung out that we are prone to getting injured, or becoming sick ourselves. I remember coming down with a cold and feeling a sense of relief and gratitude that my body was making me stay in bed. *But why must we have to get sick to rest, especially women?*

Why does self-care seem like some luxurious selfish act? When we feel reluctance to get a massage or take a long bath, our self-care becomes an opportunity for self-growth—don't we deserve to take a break? Why do we put the happiness of others before our own, while believing we have to do it all?

When we're on an airplane, if the oxygen masks come down, we are instructed to secure our own first in order to help others, because there's just no way to help anyone else unless we survive.

Desperately needing a break, I arranged a long camping weekend on the McKenzie River with both of my daughters. Since I had my younger daughter, the mental health counselor, captive in the car for three hours, I asked about her theory on self-care. Although I had been doing such interviews with her for over a year for this book, this girl never ceases to amaze me with the depth of wisdom she carries around in her big, beautiful twenty-nine-year-old heart.

During our drive, I learned that self-care isn't limited to the physical—like walking in nature, or luxuriating in a bath—self-care is *expansive,* and includes psychological, emotional, spiritual, physical, and social aspects. My daughter explained that these five areas are not equal, and change frequently based on needs and resources; and, interestingly, sometimes one or more of these systems will need to rest.

Being a mental health professional, she chose to dive into psychological self-care first by asking me about my recent quality of thoughts. After making a few thinking sounds, I easily created a list in my head, silently surmising that my thoughts had been a mix between more positive than negative—equally real and assumptive—but catastrophic at times, especially when I was tired or hungry. Also, while writing this book, I'd been living in the wasteland of my past while simultaneously experiencing the beauty of joyous discoveries and anxiety about the future. I verbally summarized my mental rant by simply sharing that my thoughts have been *a mixed bag.* She then said becoming more aware of "thought migration," and bringing myself to the present while finding the positive, is the key to psychological self-care—which I think I will be working on for the rest of my life.

Her excitement about emotional self-care was obvious by the way she sat up straighter in the passenger seat when she started asking questions about my feelings. She asked if I was validating myself, acknowledging how I was feeling in any given moment, and allowing my feelings space and time to process. At this point, I chose not to go into detail, because my answers would definitely warrant further exploration. While appreciating her willingness to put on her therapist hat, I wanted her just to be my smart daughter without offering solutions, as I had come to realize the job I was doing with emotional self-care in my burned out state was not good.

Diving into spiritual self-care with the enthusiasm of someone who was sharing a big secret, she said spiritual self-care isn't always about religion. If someone is faith-based, spiritual self-care is when they are engaging with,

and happily participating in, faith-based practices. Faith-based or not, she said people aren't practicing spiritual self-care if their lives are not aligned with their values. She also said it's important to know if your values are yours, or were given to you by someone else. This reminded me of my teenage and young adult years, when I valued being perceived of as worthy of love, which had stopped working for me about a decade ago. Thank goodness values grow and shift.

Finally, she spoke about social self-care by explaining it's the *quality*, not the quantity, of social relationships (platonic or romantic) that matter. She went on to speak about the boundaries of social and alone time, and how important it is to identify if friends and partners are supportive or toxic. Having finally arrived at choosing to surround myself with people who are positive and inspiring, I felt like I had completed this part of the self-care puzzle.

After the camping trip, in a bold statement of self-care, I told my supervisor I had to let go of my case management position, and also needed to cut my hours back to part time because the health of my mind and body depended on doing so. Gratefully, I am now working twenty hours per week, and adjusting well to less income. This act of self-care afforded me the time to write my memoir, fully rested.

Bringing myself to the present while finding the positive is the key to psychological self-care—which I think I will be working on for the rest of my life.

Catharsis

Where do uncomfortable emotions go when we don't acknowledge them? They can filter into our bodies as pain or sickness, be saved as rage for later, or we end up crying in the cereal aisle at the market for what seems like no reason.

The mallet came down hard on the tip of the index finger of my right hand as I was laying laminate flooring in my dining room without help. Surprising myself, I didn't swear, gush any kind of end of the world statements, or throw my toolbox through the dining room window. Standing there in silent awe over the exquisite pain pulsating in my hand, I calmly stared at my purpling finger, then whispered softly to myself. *So this is what this kind of pain feels like.*

Conversely, a week or two later, while rushing through errands on a day off, I tried to get out of my car with the seatbelt still attached, and upon finally breaking free, bumped my head on the sun visor. It didn't hurt, but having become quite upset, I was unable to walk across the parking lot to the bank and had to get back in my car, where I pounded on the steering wheel and cried.

My mental health counselor daughter has conceived a practical and useful concept that explains my two different reactions, and says when we avoid negative emotions which have come into awareness, they will go into our *Emotional Waiting Room*. "If the room gets too full, some are prone to erupt when triggered. Triggers are initial warning signs that something in your emotional waiting room has come to the surface, or maybe your emotional waiting room is too full and can't fit another damn thing."

According to my daughter, if someone is always in a bad mood, they must have unresolved feelings about something. "If you don't feel some contentment during the day, an emotion is talking and wants your attention."

I didn't see my discontent as a teenager and young adult as being a sign of anything, and just felt miserable most of the time—unless I was intoxicated. In my adult life, I didn't feel at ease unless I ran ten miles in between swimming workouts and aerobic classes, although that irritating current of angst I often felt in my chest was a timebomb waiting for the right trigger to release it.

Where do uncomfortable emotions go when we don't acknowledge them? They can filter into our bodies as pain or sickness, be saved as rage for later, or we end up crying in the cereal aisle at the market for what seems like no reason.

If I become irritable and don't acknowledge it by stuffing it down, there will always be a consequence. That irritability will settle into my emotional waiting room, simmering, just waiting for the right moment to come back and burn me—often in the form of back pain or crying at the drop of a hat. I've learned that the emotion of any situation will always pass, especially when I acknowledge it, and am able to be with it.

My daughter says, "We need a plan to deal with our negative emotions, or a plan to not let the trigger bother us anymore. Acknowledging means talking about them, feeling them, and releasing them in healthy ways."

I clearly understand now how in my past I tried numbing the emotions of grief, shame, fear, and disappointment with staying busy, exercise, and booze. It's painful to feel these things, but whenever I've tried to numb my feelings, I've also numbed joy, happiness, and gratitude.

How do we get negative emotions out of our emotional waiting room so we can make space for more joy? We have to allow ourselves to actually *feel* our sadness, anger, or frustration, and discover ways of expressing it in compassionate ways. Creating art and writing my life story are two ways I've been allowing myself to feel, and consequently, heal.

Now, if I find myself with a feeling of angst or discontent, I pause, then ask myself out loud, *"What's wrong?"* This gives me a minute between the trigger and my reaction so I can be less reactive. It also enables me to ask myself what I need, if what I am feeling is actually true, and what the likelihood is of something bad really happening. Although I may get impatient for the answer, one will usually come—if not in that moment, very soon.

Creating art and writing my life story are two ways I've been allowing myself to feel, and consequently, heal.

NESS

I have been told on numerous occasions not to be so sensitive, or so emotional, which to me actually means don't be yourself.

I am a deeply sensitive, empathic, and intuitive individual, so it makes sense that my daughters are too.

When approaching a new environment, person, or situation, I've taught them to do what we call a *NESS* check, by dropping thought and tuning into themselves to see if they feel an immediate understanding of the positiveness, negativeness, sadness, happiness, or the *anythingness* of what they are faced with.

Once, when the three of us pulled into a hotel parking lot in Portland, my then thirteen-year-old daughter got out of the car, took two steps toward the monstrous concrete building with a green neon sign, then stopped abruptly before stating with certainty, "Mom, we can't stay here, this place has bad NESS." After calmly exploring her feelings about this hotel, I honored them, then drove down the road to another hotel, where she felt *safeness*.

Nurturing my daughters to pay attention to their intuitive nature has gifted them with believing in their instincts; and, consequently, I have cultivated a deeper sense of my own intuition.

During a different trip, we sat on a park bench while having lunch and did *NESS* checks on people walking by. We weren't judging anyone for their appearance, but were tuning into how we felt when they passed us. My daughters and I agreed that a middle-aged woman was sad, although she wore no frown. We sensed predatoriness from a young man, kindness from an elderly homeless lady, and lovely energies from a young mother. Together, we developed a great sense of how others were feeling by tuning in.

Most people do *NESS* checks without realizing it, like when we immediately scan new environments for threats to our safety, expanding or contracting as a result.

I've also learned how I feel after being with people is a good example of intuition guidance—if I'm tired, or drained, after spending time with someone I've just met, that may be a sign they are carrying negative NESS. We've all experienced what many refer to as *energy vampires,* those who seem to have a way of sucking the life out of people. Conversely, if my spirits are lifted by being with someone, that person probably has positive NESS. Intuitive, empathic people are also like sponges, and often absorb the energies of others.

I have been told on numerous occasions not to be *so sensitive,* or *so emotional*, which to me actually means *don't be yourself.*

Indeed, I *am* sensitive to the noise of crowds, to inconsiderately loud neighbors, and to sarcastic people (even if they are joking), as well as to neighboring dogs that constantly bark out of loneliness. And if I haven't been practicing good self-care, I can become overwhelmed by the painful emotions of people I care about, or have my nerves frayed when people talk excessively. I can't watch violent movies because I feel the pain of the victims in my body, and I get a moderate jolt of adrenaline when I see someone hurt themselves in "funny" home videos—those compilations of people falling off things, or getting hit in the crotch by innocent kids swinging a baseball bat, can actually cause me to double me over in pain if I'm in a fragile state.

Where did those sensitivities come from? Probably from growing up in a loud, chaotic home, where my siblings and I were all in survival mode, and did not receive the love, attention, or guidance we needed.

However, being an empath means I am also an excellent listener, a loyal friend and partner, and I always show up for people who are in crisis. Setting boundaries by controlling how much time I spend listening to stressful people, or in environments that

When people tell me they are a basket case, super critical, mad, or moody most of the time, I believe them. People generally let us know right up front who they really are—if we are present enough to notice.

---

overwhelm me—while honoring my need for alone time to recharge—has been an essential part of my learning process.

Because I now value my sensitive nature, if someone else doesn't, that is their problem. I am only willing to be myself.

A technique that I have nearly perfected, and which I use to protect myself from negativity that may be aimed in my direction (or from the triggers of stressful environments and stressful people), is one that I employ before entering a hospital or the home of a hospice patient: After making the sound of a bubble popping, I visualize a human-sized bubble in front of me, which I then step into. I refer to this as my *love bubble* because it is egg shaped and has wobbly, bubble-like edges—but it can only be permeated by love.

Part of the visualization is that no other emotion can reach me, or exude from me, which makes my love bubble absolutely invaluable.

But please understand, I haven't always carried around a love bubble, or always been able to tune into my intuition. I've learned how illogical or analytical thinking can override my intuition—which is where I got into trouble as a teenager and in early adulthood. During this time I was like a lightning rod for people who were waving red flags, although loneliness got in the way of my recognizing them, even if they were right in front of my face.

In my forties I met a man who was sweet, tender, very loving, and within the first month of dating told me point blank, "I'm not partner material." I didn't believe him though, even after he shared stories of low self-esteem, a recent suicide attempt, and his lack of drive to get ahead in life. He showed me his red flags right up front, but I couldn't see them. I was wearing rose-colored glasses that I thought were lifesaving, and was not in tune with my gut. Consequently I ended up spending over five years in relationship with him. I've often wondered if by recognizing my own pain in the way he expressed his, there was a familiarity in being with him that kept us together.

Now, I completely trust my gut, and am much less colorblind. When people tell me they are a basket case, super critical, mad, or moody most of the time, I believe them. People generally let us know right up front who they really are—if we are present enough to notice.

The Stages of Change

Depending upon my readiness for change, and knowing I can't force its momentum, I find relief in knowing that trying to change before I am ready would be like trying to push a river in a direction it isn't meant to flow in.

Unless we are scared straight into doing things differently, it is predictable that most of us will only change when we are ready.

With no groundbreaking or life-altering moment in my teens and twenties impacting me enough to cause me to stop my precarious lifestyle, my evolution away from partying and carrying on with unsavory characters didn't happen until I was ready. It was as if drugs and alcohol, which worked until they didn't, were a solution to my problems only up to the point where they no longer served me.

Although I had become aware of having emotional challenges while in my thirties, it was a long time before I was ready to address them. Similarly, it took many years for me to make the decision to finally say *yes* to walking away from my marriage for good.

I have also found that just becoming aware of the need to make a change isn't always the first step either. Although I was advised to stop unhealthy behaviors like cocaine use in my late teens, I didn't want to, even though I knew it was bad for me, because I enjoyed it. Many years later, when a long-term relationship was crumbling and my beloved women friends told me they knew from the beginning the relationship wouldn't last, I felt betrayed and asked why they hadn't been honest with me up front. Knowing what I know now, I have to agree with their response: I wouldn't have heard a word of their guidance, and needed to stay in that relationship in order to understand something about myself.

I've learned I can only take in well intended advice when I am ready to hear it.

Depending upon my readiness for change, and knowing I can't force its momentum, I find relief in knowing that trying to change before I am ready would be like trying to push a river in a direction it isn't meant to flow in.

Going back to school to become a nurse had never been a conscious plan, but a moment came in my forties when it was the right thing to do. As a sidenote, a seed *had* been planted when I was ten by my grandmother, who saved the pennies from her waitressing tips for a year, rolled them up, then with a grand gesture gave them all to me to save for nursing school someday. I decided to buy roller skates with the money instead, because I wanted to be a roller derby queen when I grew up. Although my first career choice had been to become a Las Vegas show girl, falling off a stool and breaking my arm while practicing go-go dancing had caused me to become disenchanted with that idea. I'm very grateful to have taken different career choice paths as an adult.

There are five stages of change, which I learned about in graduate school, that are spot on with the changes I've made in my life. The first stage of change is called *precontemplation* (not ready for change), followed by *contemplation* (thinking about change), *preparation* (taking small steps), and *action* (jumping into the new behavior with both feet.) *Maintenance,* the final phase, is our practicing of a new behavior until it sticks. It's common to try and then fail, or to not trust yourself and backslide a little before success occurs. Believing in ourselves is what is essential for success, and once we accomplish that, we can succeed at anything we put our minds to—usually all in perfect timing.

Before my triathlon days, I was a smoker. My father's cardiovascular disease wasn't enough to make me quit, being encouraged by others to stop didn't work either—although I did try, I'd also failed many times. I knew smoking was harming my body, but I just couldn't stop.

Finally, in my late teens I went to a Schick Center in Los Angeles, where the slogan was *Quitting smoking and losing weight can be fun*; and they answered their phone with, "There is a helpful friend on the other end." It certainly felt like I needed help, and a friend, in order to succeed in this process.

My treatment began in a stifling, windowless room about the size of a refrigerator box that smelled like a wet cardboard ashtray. There were cigarette butts more than twelve inches deep on the floor that swallowed my shoes, and a narrow counter with an overflowing ashtray sitting on a thick layer of cigarette butts and ash. Having been instructed to bring my least favorite cigarettes, a crinkly pack of Paul Mall nonfilter reds, my father's favorite brand, was in my pocket. As I sat on a wooden stool, glancing at my miserable self on one side of a two-way mirror, a cheerful attendant placed an electrode on the middle finger of my right hand, instructed me to chain smoke the cigarettes with that hand until I was told to stop, then left the room and closed the door. Every time I took a puff, the electrode shocked me, with the shocks progressively increasing in intensity. There wasn't any ventilation in the little room as I puffed like the compliant girl I was, but when it became suffocating after three nonstop cigarettes, I had to get out. After meeting with a "counselor" for fifteen minutes, I paid my $69, then drove the forty minutes home—lighting up a cigarette in the car before I even got off the freeway.

Then, a moment came about a year later when I knew for sure I was done with cigarettes—it just happened, cold turkey. Once again, I was only ready when I was truly ready.

Within the last few years, I became aware of not being as capable of setting boundaries at work as I could have been, and looking back at my evolution of saying *no*, can see how the stages of change I mentioned earlier also apply in this situation: There was a time when always saying *yes* if I was needed simply seemed like the right thing to do. Turning down a complicated admission right before the end of my shift might affect my image of being indispensable, and I certainly didn't want to appear selfish or unaccommodating.

I ultimately learned, however, that by not setting boundaries I was neglecting what *really* matters, which is my emotional and physical health. While saying *no* when someone expected me to say *yes* had consequences that were rough at the start, this new ability eventually gifted me with more time to take care of myself. As an additional bonus, my new boundary setting provided a few of my coworkers with permission to do the same.

Trust Fall

It has been through the process of inquiry, and the writing of "The Great Unlearning," that I've become convinced that credit must go to my traumas for having provided me with experiences which ultimately led me to discover my strengths.

Allow was a word I wore around my fifty-year-old wrist on a brass bangle that looked like a tiny life preserver. I often fondled the small bracelet as I went about my days, sincerely chanting *faith* and *trust* to myself as I drove to work, or as I read between the lines of a self-help book that was supposed to bring me closer to some contented destination. For a long while my life felt like it was based on the *idea* of faith and trust.

During this time, when I heard a highly regarded spiritual teacher say traumatic events don't happen *to* you, they happen *for* you, I reacted with anger: How was my dysfunctional childhood *for me*? How was being raped more than once *for me*? I couldn't even begin to imagine how my obedient decision to terminate a pregnancy at seventeen was *for me*, since the memory of it haunted me for decades. I eventually came to realize, however, that in my twenties, when those traumas defined me—and when I thought those things had happened *to* me—I had been playing a passive role in my survival, and believing in my victimhood had essentially been a frame of mind.

I desperately wanted to trust that any situation I faced, good or bad, had actually been presented to assist me in becoming a better person, but I wasn't able to trust that my life unfolded the way it did in support of personal growth. It seemed absurd that my physical and emotional pain had occurred for a beneficial purpose, and learning to reframe traumatic experiences as opportunities to learn and grow was quite challenging.

It has been through the process of inquiry, and the writing of *The Great Unlearning*, that I've become convinced that credit must go to my traumas for having provided me with experiences which ultimately led me to discover my strengths.

The pain I endured helped me to become more capable of handling difficult situations, and I ultimately emerged stronger and more flexible, like a muscle, and have developed a healthy skill set which enables me to better tolerate stress.

My emotions have had to endure some pain to grow as well, and in addition to a greater appreciation for life, I've grown a deep compassion for others, along with a credibility which allows me to identify with and help people who have gone through similar traumas. The traumas I experienced have also helped me to develop sufficient intuition and understanding to avoid potentially devastating situations that are certain to cause pain.

In these ways, my traumatic childhood was an *eventual* springboard to spiritual growth.

Without my life altering childhood experiences, and, consequently, those which took place as an adult, I wouldn't have run away to Hawaii, chosen a careless lifestyle, married the man I did, or had the beautiful daughters that I now cherish. Although I can see how my positive and negative experiences have all played important roles in who I have become, I'm not quite at the point of honestly saying I wouldn't have changed a thing, but am very grateful for the outcome.

I now agree I am not a victim of what happened; and understand that I am the person I have chosen to become in large part because of those experiences. The way I respond to any situation is always my own choice, so I can choose to be a victim and suffer, or I can use my skills to perceive what occurred through an open lens which allows me to see the potential for learning and growth.

I think it was Buddha who said if you aren't sure where you are supposed to be, just look down at your feet.

As I free fall into the unknown of sharing my story with the world, do I worry about where I'll land, or who is going to catch me? The answer to that is no, because I have ample confidence in my future self always awaiting me with open arms and a loving heart, no matter what is in store.

My life is a grand trust fall.

In these ways, my traumatic childhood was an eventual springboard to spiritual growth.

Who I Am

Upon reflecting further back to childhood, I was eventually able to see how my core beliefs and value system had been shaped by the influences of family, friends, and community—as well as the favorable and unfortunate experiences of my young life.

At a women's retreat a few years ago, I was asked to share the first three core personal values that popped into my head, and responded quickly with a perky tone: "My health, honesty, and positivity."

But when the speaker said, "If I followed you around for a week, I would know for sure if those are indeed your values," my shoulders slumped forward a little in reflection of the previous week. Having not eaten as healthily as usual and only going to the gym once for a mediocre workout, then beating myself up mentally about not getting enough done while failing to acknowledge how tired I felt, my actions certainly had not matched my values.

From that embarrassing lesson I learned how the choices I make reflect who I am, and what I value.

Lucky for all of us, values can shift.

Upon reflecting further back to childhood, I was eventually able to see how my core beliefs and value system had been shaped by the influences of family, friends, and community—as well as the favorable and unfortunate experiences of my young life. The dysfunctional core beliefs that emerged ultimately dominated, molding my identity and following me well into adulthood. Not only did I feel unlovable, but I also believed the world was not safe, people were generally untrustworthy, I didn't deserve good things or relationships, and only the fittest of manipulators survived.

Never allowing anyone to catch even a glimpse of how I truly viewed the world, I was a great pretender. By compartmentalizing my angst, and always putting on a happy face, the power of this assumed identity controlled how I would be perceived, so I continued to act accordingly.

Although positive values filtered into my consciousness for over two decades, they took up residence right alongside the dregs of the negative ones. In my early twenties I began valuing athleticism and education, but still felt inadequate. When I gave birth to my daughters, I valued motherhood, but was never sure I was doing it right. I had always valued creativity, but thought I wasn't good enough.

Upon reflection, I became aware that I married the man I did because I valued security, then divorced him because I valued independence and freedom. I bought a house I really couldn't afford, because I valued the perception of being financially stable, although I was far from it. Becoming a member of an expensive fitness club came out of a desire to join the ranks of those with a more successful status, even though some of the people I worked out with shared the very same self-defeating beliefs and values.

The long-term stress from this dysfunctional approach to life finally caught up with me in my late thirties in the form of depression, mental exhaustion, and irritability.

Then, in my late thirties, when those debilitating core beliefs weren't working anymore for the person I was evolving into, my beloved sisterhood helped tip the scale with their unwavering love and support. My mindset shifted dramatically when I began to inquire into the origins of these core beliefs and values and the ways they had molded me into the person I was.

I've also learned how to best identify my current values by observing what I admire most in others, what inspires me to be a better person, and what brings me the most joy and happiness.

I feel safe now because I can trust those I have chosen to surround myself with—people who inspire me to be kind, loving, of service, genuine, honest, compassionate, and deserving of all the love I welcome in every day. And, because my actions demonstrate these values, happiness and joy are my rewards.

Why have I chosen my beloved partner to share this glorious life with? Besides loving every inch of who he is and how he shows up in the world, I recognize my own values residing within him, with this reflection nourishing and supporting us as we passionately navigate our life together.

My mindset shifted dramatically when I began to inquire into the origins of these core beliefs and values and the ways they had molded me into the person I was.

Love is Not Enough

The wounds of our upbringing and adulthood accompany us into all relationships, romantic or not, and no matter how loving a relationship may be, those little time bombs of our history wait for just the right moment to be triggered.

When I fell in love with, then married, an ill-tempered man who didn't respect me, I was certain my love would heal the childhood wounds he held in the clenched fist he often raised above his head. Eventually, though, I came to realize the wound I thought I was nurturing in him was really my own. By idealizing and overestimating the healing power of my love in that decade-long effort to mend his broken parts, I was actually sacrificing my self-worth. Although having two children together was part of the reason for staying in the marriage as long as I did, I think I just didn't love myself enough to leave him even when I realized I should.

A few years after my divorce, I fell in love with a kindhearted man who carried with him near fatal wounds received from an abusive ex-partner, and I was positive the love I offered was strong enough to alleviate his heartache from that relationship. Ultimately, however, nothing I provided was enough of a catalyst to empower him to heal himself—and although we were in love, I wasn't sure he loved himself. Added to that was the fact that we were unable to be good partners for each other because we didn't have enough in common, and his ambitions and perspective of the world were very different than mine.

What did I unlearn from these two partnerships? Love is not enough to sustain a relationship if the other vital partnership pieces aren't in place. I can't fix or change anyone else; I can only change myself by working on my own unresolved issues.

At that disappointing stage of my life, I don't think I would have been able to recognize a functional partnership because I had never experienced one, or had one modeled for me. In truth, I probably would have felt uncomfortable in a relationship that was stable.

I entered those relationships and others like them with my heart and ego, rather than with my logical mind. Still, those unions taught me that while love is a process of emotion, compatibility is more about alignment of values. Love alone cannot guarantee compatibility, it isn't powerful enough to single-heartedly rehabilitate unresolved issues of our partners, nor can it dissolve irreconcilable differences.

Learning this required many years, and an assortment of relationships.

The wounds of our upbringing and adulthood accompany us into all relationships, romantic or not, and no matter how loving a relationship may be, those little time bombs of our history wait for just the right moment to be triggered. Sadly, if we are in love with someone who doesn't know how to communicate through those triggers, the relationship is less likely to succeed.

For instance, I've been in relationships where when my partner would calmly ask for my rationale for making a simple household decision, I could feel attacked, and a nonsensical argument would ensue. Or, if my partner seemed a little quieter than usual, after speculating that something was terribly wrong, I would spiral into old painful memories of being neglected or abandoned, and then behave accordingly.

I now understand that in order to succeed in romantic relationships, we must pick someone we not only love, but a person with a compatible set of values as well as an honest and loving communication style.

Now, I'm in love with a delightful man with similar relationship goals and values to mine who also has the ability to communicate through the kinds of triggers which inevitably show up in any relationship. For the first year of our remarkable time together, I braced myself for trouble, but it never came. Although infrequent, if one of us causes a reaction in the other, we will calmly explore the nature of our triggers, then talk about them honestly and with kindness. I feel seen, heard, and understood by this lovely man.

As a hospice nurse visiting the homes of many married couples, I ask the same question of every twosome who have been together for more than a couple of decades: *What is the secret to a long, happy relationship?* I get all sorts of quirky answers, but the most potent reply came from a ninety-four-year-old woman who was celebrating her seventieth wedding anniversary. Her simple answer? *Pick the right person.*

I have finally picked the right person.

I now understand that in order to succeed in romantic relationships, we must pick someone we not only love, but a person with a compatible set of values as well as an honest and loving communication style.

Falling into Love

Sitting next to him, I felt little arcs of electric energy dance between my left shoulder and his right as the performer played a Bolero that forced me to close my eyes and hear it with my heart.

He was making his way through a small crowd during the intermission of a classical guitar event at Paschal Winery in Southern Oregon when I intercepted him. It had been about a year since our paths last crossed, and twelve years since we first met.

The warm hug I received from him led to the unexpected discovery of a magnificent love that broke my heart open.

He had been one of my first guitar teachers after I developed a taste for flamenco during a visit to Spain, and our mutual love for classical and Spanish guitar music kept our paths crossing for well over a decade. Because of my keen interest in photographing passionate people, I frequently took pictures of this talented man at musical venues around town, and delighted in capturing the ways he demonstrated how to be in love with a guitar, and sang with his whole body.

A week after running into him at the winery, I asked if he would play guitar at my upcoming art show in July of the same year. He agreed, then asked if I could photograph him and his flamenco troupe performing the very next day. I was overjoyed with the trade, but had no idea that three weeks later our futures would be changed forever.

Before heading out to photograph him and his troupe, I decided to break a spell of social isolation by going with the flow of whatever the day had to offer. As I walked out my door with camera in hand, I vowed out loud to accept any social invitation that felt appropriate and safe. I now refer to May 19, 2018 as *The Day of Yes*.

After an exhilarating photoshoot I received a genuine hug of gratitude, and while still in his arms, after asking how he had been, was moved by his candid response. "Since I saw you about a year ago, I got a divorce, and had my heart broken a couple of times." He could have just said he'd been fine, like most people do, but his honesty allowed me to share that my relationship of seven years had recently ended as well.

As we both started glowing with beaming smiles, he asked if he could treat me to dinner with his troupe, and my answer was *yes*. I hadn't been with such a group of dynamic people in so long, it felt like I was coming back to life. Chatting nonstop while eating burgers and fries on the balmy deck of The Brickroom in Ashland, I laughed out loud several times, filled with bliss as I shared this time with him and his friends.

After dinner, he asked me to join him and a few other musicians at a Spanish Renaissance guitar concert a couple of blocks away at the Ashland Springs Hotel. I said *yes*. Sitting next to him, I felt little arcs of electric energy dance between my left shoulder and his right as the performer played a Bolero that forced me to close my eyes and hear it with my heart.

Although I felt compelled to touch him, I didn't, for fear of being perceived as inappropriate—and, as it turned out, he had been feeling the same way.

After the show, when he invited me to join his growing posse for cocktails at the hotel bar, *yes* was my reply, and he and I sipped fancy drinks as we talked until well after midnight. I hadn't had so much fun in years, and couldn't believe I was staying up that late—with my typical bedtime before ten, I felt like a kid getting away with something.

At about 1:30 am, he asked if he could walk me to my car, and another *yes* emerged from my lips. As he wrapped his arms around me, pulling me in close for a goodnight hug, he asked if I would like to take a bike ride in the wine country with him the next weekend. Once again, I said *yes*. Halfway through that invigorating bike ride, when we stopped for a shady break under an oak tree, he

I didn't know that I was waiting for this, because I didn't even know what this was, but he burst through the doors of doubt that had convinced me I would never feel completely loved.

---

gave me an unexpected kiss. What a glorious outcome from that one day when I decided to say *yes*!

We started seeing more of each other.

As I reflect on all the times we crossed paths during those twelve years, it is clear that we were intentionally developing sweet delicate threads of connection. It was most certainly not by chance. We were both married, but as our friendship grew, we were also walking toward each other's opening hearts.

His luscious love waltzed right into my life in the most beautiful of ways, in perfect timing, because we were both ready for deep, meaningful love.

Those threads of connection have since grown into strong golden cords of a brilliant kind of consistent love I've never before received, or given. For the last three years he has told me every day, *"You are loved, you are beautiful, and you are safe."* But I had to hear this about a hundred times before his words and actions stretched my heart wide enough to take them all the way in.

Vulnerable with his heart from the beginning, he asked only for complete honesty and transparency in our relationship. I admired his courageous act of loving himself enough to show up in his entirety, although I admit to initially keeping parts of my true nature hidden, in fear they wouldn't be lovable enough for him to embrace. But because he inspires me to share my entire self, I no longer have anything to hide, and can be my goofy, wild, girly, smart, sexy self around him. And, because I let those parts shine in full view, he loves me wholeheartedly.

I didn't know that I was waiting for this, because I didn't even know what *this* was, but he burst through the doors of doubt that had convinced me I would never feel completely loved.

As my heart expands ever wider with the potential of where his love will take me, I am in full trust of this irresistibly magnificent path of growth we are on together.

Last week, I asked him to marry me, he said *yes*.

Love Fully

Receiving love hasn't always been easy for me. In fact, for many years I didn't feel worthy of it, but how could I receive love when I didn't love myself very much?

To love fully is to be brave. It has taken me years of courageous intent to love with all my heart, because in choosing to love, I have also wholeheartedly chosen the risk of heartbreak. Love and risk have also taken me hand in hand down a road of beautiful discovery to the practice of self-love.

To me, self-love is a goal of unconditional positive regard of myself regardless of my flaws, struggles, and failures.

By loving fully, I've been delivered to a depth of unimaginable love I never thought possible, with the healing journey of my heart transpiring thanks to being able to show up for my wounded self from a place of self-love and compassion that now permanently lives deep in my chest.

One way I have fostered self-love in my daughters is with a heart opening ritual we share on birthdays. Before I serve a favorite meal, we hold hands, and everyone around the table says at least one thing they love and appreciate about the person celebrating the birthday. Then, that person shares what they love and appreciate about themselves. The power of giving and receiving during this ritual always evokes tears of joy.

Receiving love hasn't always been easy for me. In fact, for many years I didn't feel worthy of it, but how could I receive love when I didn't love myself very much? And, if I couldn't love me, the person I know best, how could I offer love to other people?

It was only when I started seeing myself the way those who love me do that I attracted the love of my life and was able to receive him fully.

With my inquiry into self-love, when I asked what parts of myself are the hardest to love, the parts I would compare with the external world—like physical attractiveness, athletic abilities, and intellect—always made me come up short. I've

since become much better at not comparing myself to others, but it is still difficult to accomplish in a world that demands perfection.

During my self-loathing days, although I was offered loving gestures from people, they often came at a cost. I thought if I was given love, a kind gesture, or a material thing, I had to give something back in return. Now, because I love and respect myself, I can receive something without feeling like I'm in debt, emotionally or physically. I value reciprocation when it feels appropriate, and kindly return favors, but don't feel I owe anybody anything. I love myself enough to say yes, and enough to say no.

I'm also getting better at treating myself with understanding and forgiveness when I fail, or feel inadequate, and am learning I can make mistakes and still love who I am. Like most areas of personal growth, I am a work in progress.

Now, every time I make a mistake, as silly as it sounds, I say out loud *Oh Mary, I still love you.*

I love who I am becoming.

It was only when I started seeing myself the way those who love me do that I attracted the love of my life and was able to receive him fully.

Bloom Where You Are Planted

My difficulties setting boundaries were based on a fear of being alone, so if I didn't feel wanted, I would make myself needed in order to receive the constant validation I craved.

The last time I saw my mother was about eight years ago, at my younger brother's funeral.

At forty-eight, he had put a gun in his mouth and blew his brains out in his living room, where his wife later found him. The extreme nature of this event brought our entire family together after an estranged decade or more, and as my mother wept out loud at his funeral lamenting about the pain of losing a child, I wondered what part of that loss was the most painful for her, since she had not really been involved in his life after she recklessly kicked him out of the house when he was barely sixteen.

After the funeral, when we were all gathering in the parking lot of the mortuary to go our separate ways, my mother leaned against the trunk of her car, smiled as if she'd been told to say *cheese*, and said, "Let's forget about the past and start fresh." My four stunned siblings and I looked at each other, then at her, with the same dumbfounded voiceless resentment.

I imagine she believed she was offering us an olive branch, but her words felt as heavy as the imaginary brick I held in my hand that I wanted to toss through the back window of her car. *You don't get off the hook that easy!*

The further away from that afternoon I got, the angrier I became—with my reaction a sure sign that more work was needed to make my way through the remaining mangled web of scar tissue resulting from my childhood and adolescence.

Fast-forward to last week when I briefly thought about reaching out to my mother, which seemed like a noble thing to do with all the unlearning I'd been doing for the last two years while writing this book. I took a couple of steps toward finding out where she was, and discovered what state she was living in with her third husband, but, by the end of the day, the part of me that knows I will most likely never have a loving relationship with her talked me out of it.

Many years ago, I had let go of the irrational hope that my mother would somehow become a person I could rely on, and had come to understand how unlikely it was that she would ever even be able to have a meaningful conversation with me. Anyway, it felt like it was too late, with too much water having rushed under the bridge that separates our family.

And yet, that same week, when I kept hearing *she did the best she could* from families of hospice patients as they attempted to justify their dying parent's actions, their words gave me pause.

Did my mother do the best she could raising her children?

Doing the best you can may be a valid reason, but it's also a rotten excuse for unacceptable behavior, and using that statement to let my mother off the hook felt more like a cop-out. In my mind, I have often approached her with fangs exposed, yelling:

What's wrong with you? Why did you abandon your ill husband and six kids and treat us the way you did? You have no idea the consequences of your screwed up actions that fucked us all up!

But just as I've learned that my behaviors and wounding were a result of my unmet needs, I know that hers were too. Since my upbringing lacked physical contact, presence, companionship, listening, guidance, kindness, and displays of love, I now wondered what her unmet needs had been.

Because of my self-inquiry and explorations for this book, if I ever do see her again, and the moment feels right, I might ask her about her own childhood in order to better understand why she made the choices she did as a mother. With fangs retracted, I'd ask:

What happened to you?

Since the answer to that question explains why I chose to present myself to the world in the ways I did, it would be true for her as well. Because of my childhood experiences, it is understandable why I emerged into the world with an impaired sense of self, was overly sensitive, lacked adequate emotional intelligence, and chose toxic friends and partners. My difficulties setting boundaries were based on a fear of being alone, so if I didn't feel wanted, I would make myself needed in order to receive the constant validation I craved.

A brave moment came, and I called my mother's brother in Virginia, and her former brother-in-law in Arizona. I learned that her cold parents were often outwardly angry, rarely showed affection, and did not accept the way she expressed herself. Both uncles said she developed narcissistic tendencies into adulthood and needed to be the center of attention—which was impossible in the chaos of six young children who all needed her to focus on them.

I understand now, with all my heart, that my mother's careless behavior wasn't *about me*. It wasn't because I was unlovable. She probably didn't know how to mother other than the way she had been mothered. *Does that mean she did do the best she could?*

The process of forgiving her has been incremental, and I've blossomed in my progress over the years. I've learned that carrying around anger about my upbringing was poisonous to me, and hanging onto my anger only succeeded in giving her control over me. Forgiveness doesn't mean I have excused or dismissed her wrongdoing, nor will I forget it, but it does mean I'm letting go of my bitterness and feelings of resentment as I continue to develop more compassion for her based on what she went through.

Through my hospice work, I have seen how a terminal diagnosis can bring out the best and worst in families. When I witness adult children expressing anger toward their dying parents, I no longer wonder what is wrong with them, or why are they treating their parent that way.

Instead, I wonder, *What happened to you that caused you to feel like this?*

I am now aware that every single person I cross paths with carries around unresolved pain, especially the people who have caused me pain. By approaching everyone with this in mind, my compassion has grown, and the knowledge that everyone is a product of their upbringing remains front and center in my thoughts.

How to Save a Life

I feel honored to be called into this most sacred and vulnerable time in people's lives. I find joy in participating in deeply meaningful conversations with the dying, and in sharing the grand wisdom I receive from them.

I am a better person thanks to the time I spend with the dying.

Along with hospice nursing having helped me become more of the person I want to be, I've also been gifted with endless reminders of the value of selflessness and unconditional love, all while having my faith in human connection constantly renewed.

My patients have all been told they have six months or less to live, and along with that news comes a whirlwind of opportunities for me to help them navigate the time they have remaining. In return, I have learned how to be more present, and how to live and love more fully.

I feel honored to be called into this most sacred and vulnerable time in people's lives. I find joy in participating in deeply meaningful conversations with the dying, and in sharing the grand wisdom I receive from them.

My experiences in hospice, which provide regular wake-up calls to the temporary nature of life, have taught me to cherish precious time spent with my loved ones, as well as the preciousness of my limited time here on earth.

A terminal diagnosis is often followed by a disruption in priorities, beliefs, and values, with the news sometimes bringing out the best and worst qualities in people. Essential time spent with memories can resolve old issues if there are any, and help individuals come to terms with life choices, and take care of unfinished business—but the unresolved frequently takes center stage. I recognize my own pain in the some of the families I serve, and am therefore provided with great opportunities to examine my own unresolved issues.

I have witnessed, and wholeheartedly believe, that healing is possible while dying. I'm not referring to physical healing here, but to emotional and spiritual healing. As an instrument in helping people

(and ultimately myself) return to wholeness and self-acceptance, through coaching others I get to practice unconditionally giving and receiving love and forgiveness. With every hospice family I spend time with, there seems to be someone in the house that receives a healing, and sometimes it's me. This work has helped me cope with difficult times in my life.

I appreciate having tools of compassionate education, presence, listening, and medicine which can help make the dying process less physically and emotionally painful for patients and families, while also bringing more peace of heart and mind to everyone involved. I have clearly defined this as my unwavering purpose, and with my children having witnessed my evolution, I see them able to offer compassionate presence to those they spend time with as well.

In addition to experiencing a sense of accomplishment and meaning as an advocate for patients and families without a voice (and for those who perceive themselves as such), helping people to have as much control as possible at the end of life has also helped me to appreciate the many choices I have in my own life.

The physical and emotional tragedies that people endure in this life humble me on a regular basis. Everybody wants to be loved, although not everyone is, and I can easily bring some love into the lives of people who need it most.

If I had a closed heart, I wouldn't have the courage to ask the difficult questions that can lead a patient, or their family, down an open-hearted path of courageous exploration. Spending time with the dying and their families keeps my heart open.

Hospice work is what I am meant to do. I've been told I carry a calming presence in difficult moments which often diffuses emotionally charged environments—and by perfecting these skills gained through

I have witnessed, and wholeheartedly believe, that healing is possible while dying.

---

hospice work, I've also been able to bring them into my daily life.

Tears well up in my eyes when I say to the dying: *Your work on this planet is done, there is nothing more to do, and nowhere else to go.* I've been exploring what those tears mean, and have come to feel that they are a joyous response to the gift I can give of a powerful offer of permission for the patient to stop.

Over the years, I have asked many hospice patients for advice on how to live my best life. Since they are facing death, of course their perspective on living has shifted dramatically, and I've received some pretty good guidance.

Don't postpone happiness. Don't wait until the timing is right, when the kids are out of the house, when you have enough money, or when you are caught up. Live while you are alive, because at any minute, your life could be stopped in its tracks by disease or disability.

Stop watching TV and spend face to face time with the people you love, don't assume they know how you feel. Leave your comfort zones and take risks for love. One of the significant regrets of the dying is that they can't go back and create happy loving memories with the ones they are leaving behind.

Work less. Nobody has ever said to me on their deathbed that they wished they would have worked more.

Get out of the house. Play, be curious, take walks, dance, appreciate nature, and travel. Many dying people say they always had an intention to play and explore, but never found the time.

Be happy, love, and play is very good advice indeed.

The Second Beginning

Over twenty-five years ago, and many times between then and now, one of my dearest sister friends shared a profound philosophy with me that has finally driven me home.

Show up present and vulnerable, speak your compassionate truth, ask for exactly what you want, and ignore the outcome. What you want is wanting for you.

The magnificent and miraculous outcome of her life-altering advice is this book, and the phenomenal healing I have been gifted by being brave enough to find out what was in my way of loving myself enough to ask for what I want.

As it turns out, what I wanted was wanting for me.

About the Author

Award winning photographer and author of three inspiring books, Mary La (formerly Mary Landberg), is a joyful hospice RN who carries a camera in her nursing bag. She offers free portraiture to hospice families, which led to the publishing of her book *Enduring Love: Inspiring Stories of Love and Wisdom at the End of Life*. This heartwarming book is a collection of over one hundred black and white portraits of hospice patients with family and friends embracing love and life. Included are grand love stories, inspiring conversations with the dying, their advice for living, and the wisdom their illnesses have gifted them. She is at work on her next hospice portraits book, *The Last I Love You*.

Mary holds a Bachelor of Science in exercise science and a Master's in Public Health, with a focus in community health program development and implementation. For the last thirty years she has been teaching, coaching, and promoting healthy lifestyles to diverse multicultural audiences in community, corporate, and collegiate environments.

Her writing and photographic adventures began when she was inspired to go back to school at the age of forty-three to earn credentials in nursing. While in nursing school, Mary published *Fear Means Go*, a book of mind-opening poetry and photography, which reflects an inspiring ten-year journey of reflection, self-discovery, and evolution. From looking in all the wrong places for love, settling for less, and enduring relationships often driven by loneliness and lack, Mary offers opportunities for healing and shares the gifts that her suffering revealed while taking risks to fully expose her authentic self.

From the *Fear Means Go* experience, *Photography for the Uninhibited* was born, a dynamic portraiture service capturing the authentic spirit and passion of the fearless self. Please check out her photography at **www.photographyfortheuninhibited.com**

While documenting the hero's journey of her life while in her early fifties, she was led to the cathartic powers of surreal conceptual portraiture and created *The Great Unlearning: A unique memoir of inspiring self-portraits and incredible, true stories of transcendence.*

To learn more about Mary's books, or to schedule a speaking engagement, please visit **www.Mary-La.com**

www.ingramcontent.com/pod-product-compliance
Lightning Source LLC
Chambersburg PA
CBHW061805290426
44109CB00031B/2936